M. M. Runciman

Rules of Perspective

Explained, Illustrated, and Adapted to Practical Use

M. M. Runciman

Rules of Perspective
Explained, Illustrated, and Adapted to Practical Use

ISBN/EAN: 9783337050207

Printed in Europe, USA, Canada, Australia, Japan

Cover: Foto ©Suzi / pixelio.de

More available books at **www.hansebooks.com**

RULES OF PERSPECTIVE.

EXPLAINED, ILLUSTRATED, AND ADAPTED

TO PRACTICAL USE.

BY

M. M. RUNCIMAN.

WITH LETTER OF APPROVAL

FROM

PROFESSOR JOHN RUSKIN, M.A., HON. LL.D., &c. &c.

𝕬rs probat artificem.

LONDON:

WINSOR & NEWTON, Limited, 38, RATHBONE PLACE, W.

Owing to the difficulties in binding, the Vanishing and Station Points on the folding plates may not be found accurately true; but the letterpress fully explains all that is necessary.

CONTENTS.

4th June 84

Dear Miss Runciman

I assure you it gave
me true pleasure to see your
writing again; and to learn
that you had made the
alterations suggested in the
arrangement of your Father's
rules, — before not wholly clear
Your having done so enables
me at once to guarantee the
scientific accuracy and easy
applicability of the rules; and
with the greater security — because
I myself learned all the perspective
from them which I ever apply
to landscape practice
Believe me always,
Your faithful Serv ts
John Ruskin

PREFACE.

IT has always seemed to me that Perspective, to beginners, is so difficult to understand, that the amateur either lays it aside in despair, or, what is worse, tries to draw by eye what was never correctly done but by rule.

I have therefore explained, and illustrated, as simply as possible, the following Rules, taught by my father, Charles Runciman, who was Mr. Ruskin's first drawing master.

They are all the artist will find necessary for interior, or landscape drawing, to which Mr. Ruskin has kindly affixed his Certificate of their rightness.

MERCY M. RUNCIMAN.

49, ACACIA ROAD,
  ST. JOHN'S WOOD, N.W.

.

EXAMPLE 1.—DIRECTIONS FOR DRAWING A CUBICAL BOX.

Draw the nearest, or most important, perpendicular line.

By its length determine the relative height of the eye, by holding the ruler even with the eyes, and finding (as an approximation) how many of these lines continued upwards it will take to give the height of the eye.

Draw the horizontal line at the height of the eye.

Place on the horizontal line your point of sight, *always in the centre of your picture.*

Fix the station point, which must be under the point of sight, and removed from it a distance equal to the length of the picture.

Find your vanishing points by placing your ruler at your station point, parallel with one side of your box, until the ruler intersects the horizontal line, which determines the first vanishing point: the second is obtained by taking a right angle at the station point, until the ruler intersects the horizontal line, which will give the second vanishing point.

For the length of the lines forming the sides of the box, draw a measuring line, as by Example A: mark on it the proportions required.

Find the dividing point, by placing the ruler at the vanishing point, and measuring the distance from it to the station point, and laying that distance on the horizontal line, measured from the vanishing point. The same rule applies to both sides of the box.

EXAMPLE 1.

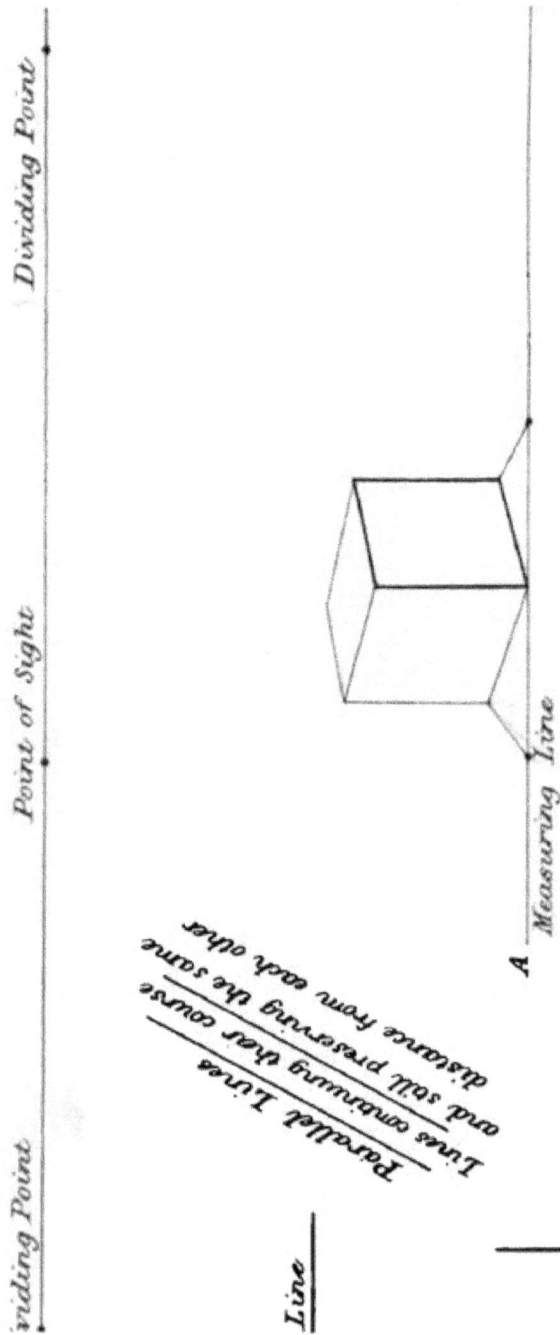

Dividing Point

Point of sight

Dividing Point

A   Measuring Line

Parallel Lines
Lines continuing their course
and still preserving the same
distance from each other

Line

Right Angle

EXAMPLE 2.—FOR DRAWING A CUBICAL BOX IN PARALLEL PERSPECTIVE.

Draw the size of the box required, find the height of the eye, the horizontal line, point of sight (*always in the centre of the picture*), and station point, as by Example 1.

All lines parallel to each other in nature must be drawn to the same vanishing point.

In parallel perspective the point of sight becomes the vanishing point: as by Example 2. The measuring line and dividing point must be used to give the length of the lines in perspective. In sketching from nature, the simplest cottage cannot be drawn without the rules given in Examples 1 and 2. And although the artist may say that ruler and compasses are a great incumbrance, still, the knowledge of how to apply the rules will give a more truthful result even without the ruler: a long slip of paper will be found to make a fair substitute. First, then, the size of your picture must be determined, placing the horizontal line at the height

EXAMPLE 2.

Point of sight

Horizontal line

Measuring line

of the eye (on level ground) about a third of the height of your picture. If standing on high ground, the horizontal line will be higher accordingly. Place your point of sight in the middle of your picture and on the horizontal line, your station point under it, a distance equal to the length of the picture. If your ruler be placed at the station point, parallel (or even with) one side of the building you wish to draw in perspective, then a right angle at the station point will give the other vanishing point on the horizontal line.

Draw in your building by the vanishing points, as by Example 3, remembering that all lines parallel will vanish to the same point.

EXAMPLE 4—Gives an Illustration of Parallel Perspective.

EXAMPLE 4.

EXAMPLE 3.

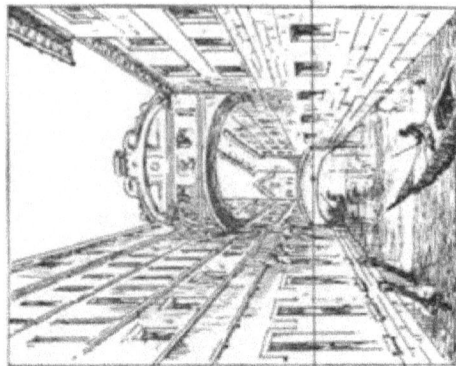

Vanishing Point.

Example 3.

Horizontal line
Example 4

In Parallel Perspective, the point of sight becomes the vanishing point to which both sides of the building are drawn.

EXAMPLE 5.—AN INTERIOR, DRAWN IN PERSPECTIVE.

Drawing an interior by perspective is often thought very difficult; but the simple rule used in drawing a cubical box (Example 1) is all that is necessary. First, as in the case of the box, draw the most important perpendicular line, say the corner of the room you wish to sketch (O), which had better not be in the centre of your paper, as, artistically, it is most agreeable to the eye that the sides of the room should not be equal in length. By its length determine the height of the eye. Place your horizontal line at the height of your eye, and on it the point of sight in the centre of your picture, your station point under it, a distance equal to the length of the picture. Put your ruler at the station point, parallel (or even with) one side of the room, and where your ruler intersects the horizontal line decides the first vanishing point; the second is obtained by taking a right angle at the station point until the ruler intersects the horizontal line, which will give the second vanishing point. Draw in your room, using the two vanishing points, as by Example 5.

EXAMPLE 5.

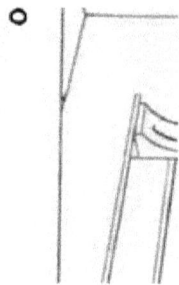

EXAMPLE 6.—STEPS, IN PERSPECTIVE.

The same rule as in drawing a cubical box (Example 1) again applies. First, the nearest perpendicular line must be drawn, by its length the height of the eye determined, the horizontal line—at the height of the eye, point of sight, station point, and vanishing points. Draw a horizontal measuring line at the base of the nearest perpendicular line, as by Example 6. Find your dividing points by measuring the distance from the vanishing point to the station point, and laying that distance on the horizontal line, measured from the vanishing point. Then decide how many steps you wish to draw; if four, divide your measuring line into four equal parts, and by using your dividing points, carry the size of each step back to the block as by 1, 2, 3, 4, which will give the true size of each step in perspective. Then continue the nearest perpendicular line, so as to form a perpendicular measuring line, as by 7; mark on it the height of each step, and draw your steps in, using the two vanishing points as in Example 6.

EXAMPLE 6.

EXAMPLE 7.—DRAWN BY THE SAME RULE AS EXAMPLE 6.

EXAMPLE 7.

Point of

EXAMPLE 8.—TO DRAW STAIRS, UP AND DOWN, IN PARALLEL PERSPECTIVE.

Decide the size of your picture, the height of your eye, the horizontal line, point of sight, station point, and vanishing point. The stairs being in parallel perspective, the point of sight becomes the vanishing point. Draw your first step the length and width you wish it: the length in parallel perspective is easily determined; the width must be found by using your dividing point, as by 9. The rule for a dividing point being — to find your vanishing point, measure the distance from it to the station point, and lay that distance on the horizontal line, in parallel perspective the point of sight being the vanishing point. To give the inclined line to which the stairs vanish, use the rule given for the vanishing point of an inclined line, and draw an inclined line from 7 and 8, then use your square to give the perpendicular lines, and your vanishing point until it intersects the inclined line, which will give the width of the stairs. For drawing stairs down, put a measuring line, 1, 2, 3, 4, mark on it the height of the stairs, and draw to the vanishing point. The width of the stairs is determined by marking on the measuring line the width required, and by using the dividing point the desired width will be given in perspective.

EXAMPLE 8.

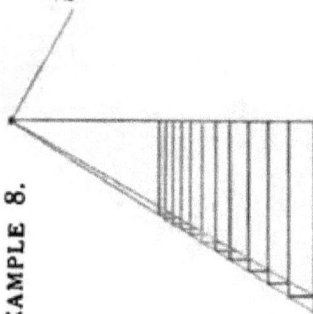

Vanishing point of inclined *line*

For the vanishing point of an inclined line, find the vanishing point on the horizontal line, to which the inclined line would have been drawn if it had been horizontal. Pass a perpendicular line through that point, then continue the inclined line till it intersects the perpendicular. The intersection is the vanishing point required.

EXAMPLE 9.

In order to draw a circle in perspective, it is necessary to enclose it in a square, so that the square being drawn in any position, the circle can then be placed in perspective. In Fig. 1 the square is not in perspective. The necessary intersections are given by a line from corner to corner, a line through the centre, horizontally and perpendicularly, dividing one side into seven. Draw a line at 2 and 3, which will give the intersection for the circle required.

Fig. 4 is drawn horizontally, and in parallel perspective. The point of sight in parallel perspective being the vanishing point, the dividing point must be used to obtain the line 5, until it intersects line 6.

For a dividing point, find the vanishing point of the line to be divided, measure the distance from it to the station point, and lay that distance on the horizontal line, measured from the vanishing point.

EXAMPLE 9.

Point of sight _____ Horizontal line

Fig. 4.

Line 6

5

EXAMPLE 10.

To turn a circle in perspective, the square which encloses it must first be drawn according to previous rules—namely, the horizontal line placed even with the height of the eye, the point of sight, station point, and vanishing points found, a measuring line put at the nearest corner of the square, as by Fig. 1, the right proportion marked on it, and the dividing point used to give lines 2, 3, and 4, which decides the 7th in perspective. A line from corner to corner, and through the centre, will determine the intersections through which the circle must be turned.

Fig. 5 is drawn by putting the square into perspective (by previous rules), and so obtaining the circle.

For a dividing point, find the vanishing point of the line to be divided, measure the distance from it to the station point, and lay that distance on the horizontal line, measured from the vanishing point.

EXAMPLE 10.

Dividing point   Point of sight   Dividing point

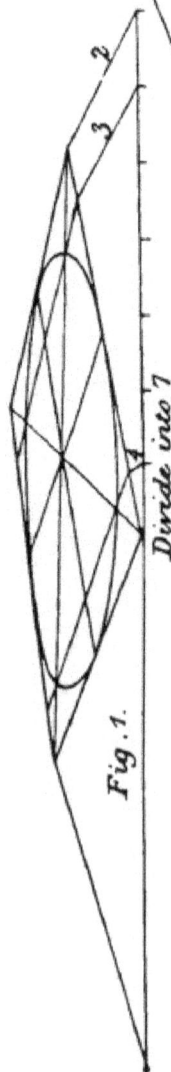

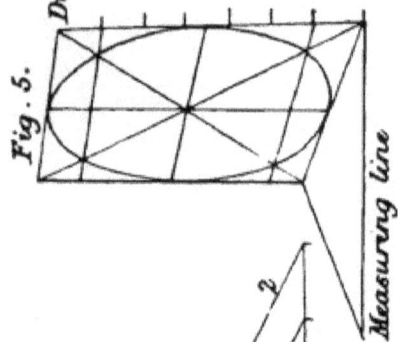

Fig. 5.

Divide into 7

Measuring line

Divide into 7

Fig. 1.

EXAMPLE II.

A bridge, consisting of a succession of semicircular arches, can only be rightly drawn when each arch is placed in by the rules of perspective. The bridge itself must therefore first be drawn by the same rule as Example I. The height of the first arch must be decided, and marked on the nearest perpendicular line, from A to B. A measuring line must then be put at the base, and the required proportions marked on it. The width of each arch would be twice its height. Find the dividing point, and use it to carry the true size of the half square back to the model. Form a half square, as from 5 to 6. A line through the centre, and from corner to the centre, will give the necessary intersection. This must be repeated for each arch. It may be said that drawing the circles in perspective would take too much time in sketching from nature ; but the knowledge of how to do them correctly would give a power of drawing them by eye at least more truthfully.

To carry the arch through to the other side of the bridge, use the two vanishing points, as by Example II.

See the rule for finding a dividing point on the previous page.

EXAMPLE II.

p^t 5   6

EXAMPLE 12.

To draw round towers, first determine the size of your picture, the horizontal line at the height of the eye, the point of sight in the centre of your picture, the station point, and the vanishing point, which in parallel perspective is the point of sight. Find the dividing point, by measuring the distance from the vanishing point to the station point, and laying that distance on the horizontal line. Draw the perpendicular sides of the tower, A and B, put a horizontal line from C to D, which will give the diameter; pass a line from the dividing point through the centre of that line, which will cut the sides of the square drawn from the vanishing point, and so decide the size of the square which encloses the circle. Complete the square, find the 7th (as by previous rules for circles), and draw the circle through the intersections, as by Fig. 2, Example 12. The same rule applies to towers not in the centre of the picture, which will appear true if the eye be opposite to the point of sight.

EXAMPLE 12.

Fig. 1.

Fig. 2.

Fig. 3.

EXAMPLE 13.

Draw the tower, and first half-circle, A, by rules on previous page. To obtain the second whole circle, form a new square removed from A the distance required, the horizontal line in the centre of the new square being the same as A, but extended as far as found necessary. Draw the crown of the tower, C; find the half-circle for the base of the turrets by previous rules.

To draw the turrets in perspective, put a circular measuring line, D, mark on it the proportions required, and use them as by Example 13. The thickness of the turrets to be drawn to the centre of the line, C. The circular measuring line would be the same if the towers were placed to the right or left, for since the squares forming the intersections for the circle are in parallel perspective, the circular measuring line would be so also.

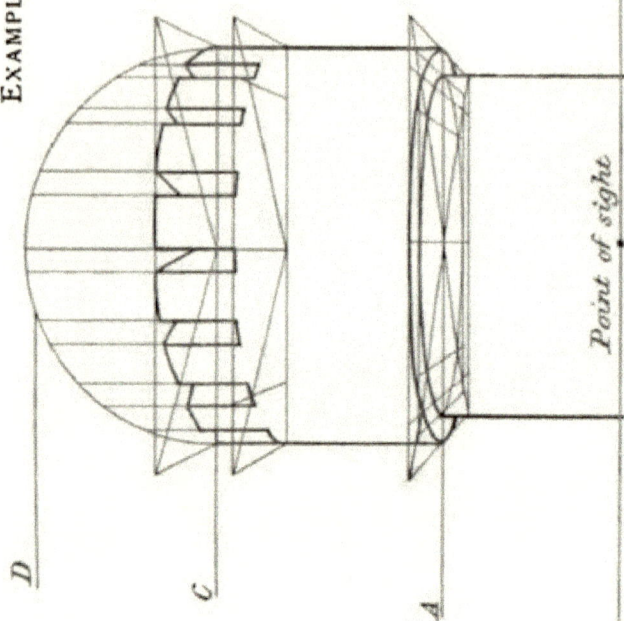

EXAMPLE 13.

D

C

A

Point of sight

EXAMPLE 14.

Draw a box by previous directions, Example 1. For the vanishing point of the inclined line given by the open lid, find that vanishing point on the horizontal line to which the inclined line would have been drawn had it been horizontal. Pass a perpendicular line through that point. Then continue the inclined line until it intersects the perpendicular. The intersection is the vanishing point required. For determining the fourth of the circle on which the lid moves from the hinge, place the size of the side of the box the lid fits (taken from the measuring line) A to B. Draw the quarter-square as by Example 14: the quarter-circle thus obtained will decide the determination of the inclined line of the lid. For giving the further inclined line, draw the top of the box as seen through, which will decide the hinge from which the inclined line starts. Draw the inclined line to the vanishing point found for the inclined lines ; for since all lines parallel continue their course to the same point, the vanishing point would be the same as the first inclined line was drawn to.

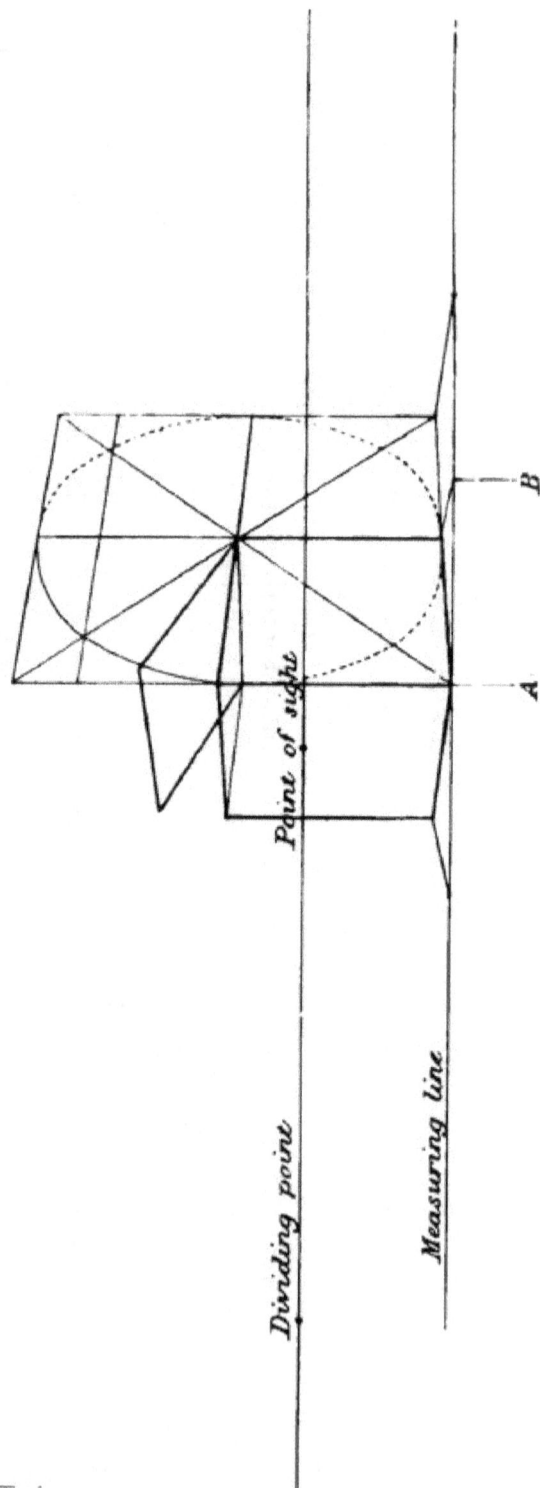

EXAMPLE 14.

Dividing point

Point of sight

Measuring line

A

B

EXAMPLE 15.

First draw a cubical box, as by Example 1. Draw the inclined line as by directions on the previous page. For the thickness of the lid of the box, A, B, C, D, find that vanishing point on the horizontal line to which the inclined line would have been drawn had it been horizontal; pass a perpendicular through the point, B, then continue the inclined line, until it intersects the perpendicular. The intersection is the vanishing point of the inclined line of the lid. For the thickness, continue that line from the vanishing point of the inclined line until it meets the horizontal line. A right angle at that juncture carried back on to the perpendicular line, will give the vanishing point required for the thickness of the lid drawn in any position. Example 15 is to show the use of the circles in deciding the length of the inclined line of the lid of a box. The knowledge of the laws respecting circles is invaluable in drawing the domes of cathedrals, round towers, water-wheels, the length of the sails of mills, or wherever a true circle is needed ; and, in interiors, for round tables, bowls for flowers, vases, &c. &c., which cannot possibly be truly drawn without these laws.

EXAMPLE 15.

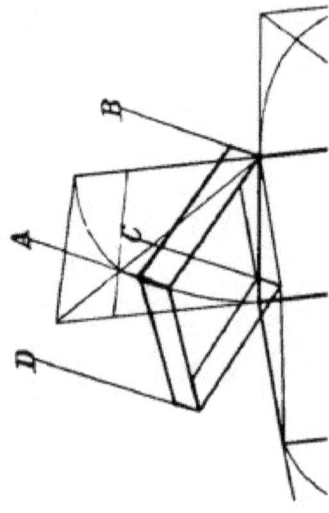

A
B
C
D

Dividing point

EXAMPLE 16.

A floor cloth of alternate light and dark squares must be placed in by the same rule as Example 1—namely, to decide the size of the picture, the horizontal line, point of sight, which in parallel perspective (as Example 16) becomes the vanishing point. Find the dividing point by measuring the distance from the point of sight to the station point, and laying that distance on the horizontal line, measured from the point of sight. Draw the square that is nearest A by the vanishing point, and measure on the measuring line the size your squares are to be. Repeat that size on the measuring line for as many squares as your floor cloth requires, then use the dividing point to the squares in the centre of your picture, which will give the retiring size of each square in perspective. Horizontal lines continued from these squares will decide all the others.

EXAMPLE 16.

EXAMPLE 17.

The floor cloth in Example 17 is not in parallel perspective, but each square having its two vanishing points. The first square must be drawn with the use of the dividing point to obtain the true square in perspective; the horizontal line at the base of the picture, being the measuring line on which the size of the square first drawn, and the others in succession, are determined by the use of the dividing points. Use alternately the vanishing points and dividing points. One line of squares being found will give all the rest, drawing with the dividing point from the measurement on the measuring line. The above rule is useful in placing the pattern of a carpet, or tesselated pavement, &c. &c.

EXAMPLE 17.

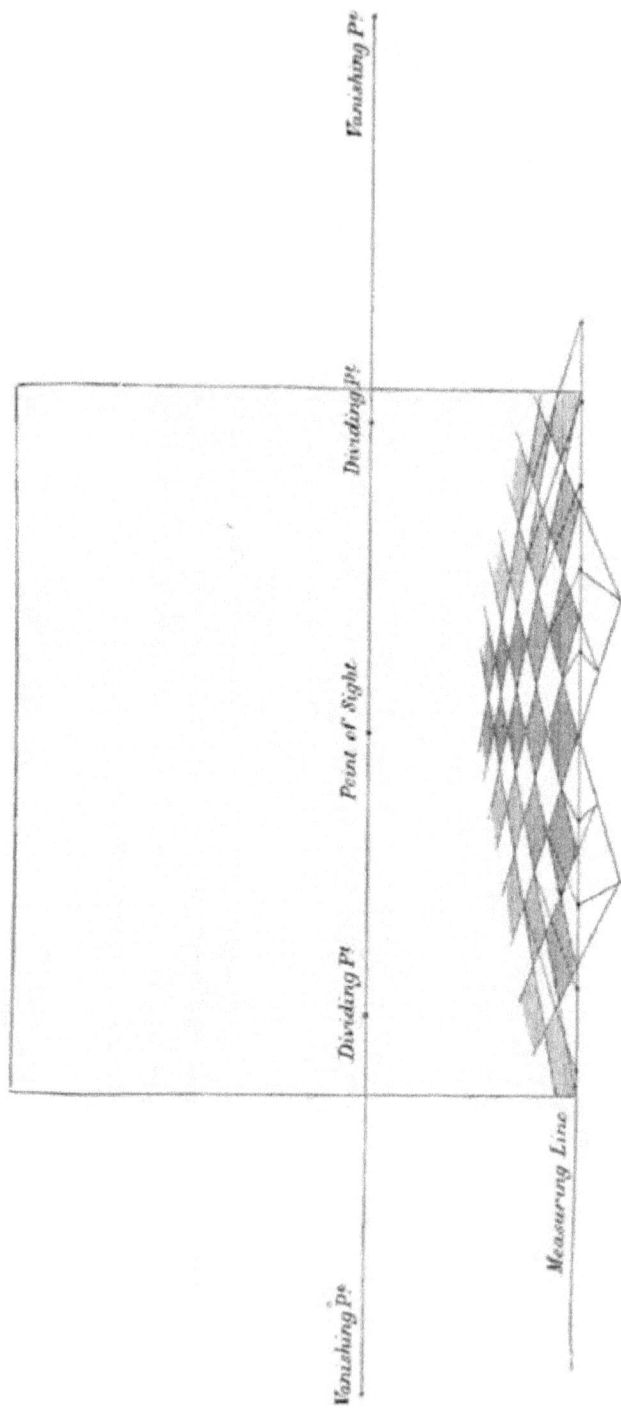

Vanishing Pt.

Dividing Pt.

Point of Sight

Dividing Pt.

Vanishing Pt.

Measuring Line

EXAMPLE 18.

In drawing an open door, it is necessary that it should be of such a size, that when closed it will fit the doorway. The following simple rule will make this easy:—First, draw the perpendicular line, A; by its length, decide the height of the eye, the horizontal line, point of sight, which must be in the middle of the picture and on the horizontal line. Next, the station point, placed at a distance equal to the length of your picture from the point of sight: place the ruler at the station point, parallel with one side of the room you intend to draw, and where it intersects the horizontal line is the vanishing point of the side of the room. The vanishing point for the other side of the room is given by taking a right angle at the station point from the first vanishing point, and where it cuts the horizontal line decides the second vanishing point. So far, it is exactly the same as the rule for drawing a cubical box (Example 1). For the doorway, draw it the size it appears in nature, pass a measuring line through the hinge, and find the dividing point of the doorway by measuring from its vanishing point to the station point, and laying that distance on the horizontal line. Then draw a line by the dividing point, from the corner of the top of the doorway to the measuring line, which will give the true size of the doorway on the measuring line. Then take a fresh vanishing point on the horizontal line for the door, and by it draw the top and the bottom of the door; and for the length of these lines, find the dividing point of the *door*, by measuring from the vanishing point of the

EXAMPLE 18.

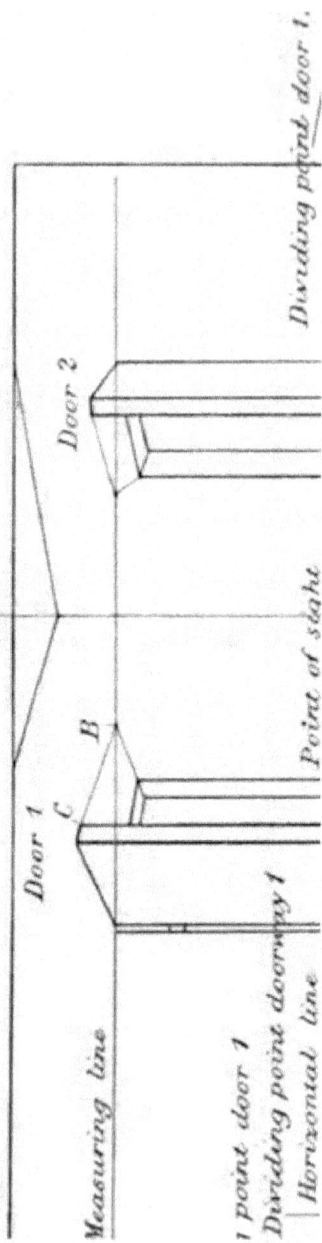

Door 1

Door 2

A

C
B

Measuring line

1 point door 1
Dividing point doorway 1
Horizontal line

Point of sight

Dividing point door 1.

door to the station point, and laying that distance on the horizontal line. Then draw from the measurement on the measuring line B, by the dividing point to C, and that will give the desired width of the door, as by Example 18. The same rule applies to both doors.

The foregoing rules will be found to comprise all that is most needed in sketching from nature, whether for interior or outdoor work, and can be adapted to much that is found difficult without. For instance, there is perspective needed in giving the size of figures in a picture.

Take the height of a man to be eight heads high, place the figure the height you wish it to be in the foreground of the picture; a line taken from the top of the head and again at the feet, drawn to the point of sight, will give the size of the figure throughout the picture. There is perspective in clouds, in trees—indeed, the adaptation of it is endless, and unless the artist has some knowledge of its principles he cannot draw truthfully the humblest object. It is to be hoped, therefore, that the rules contained in this little pamphlet may be found helpful. They, at least, have the merit of being easy and true.

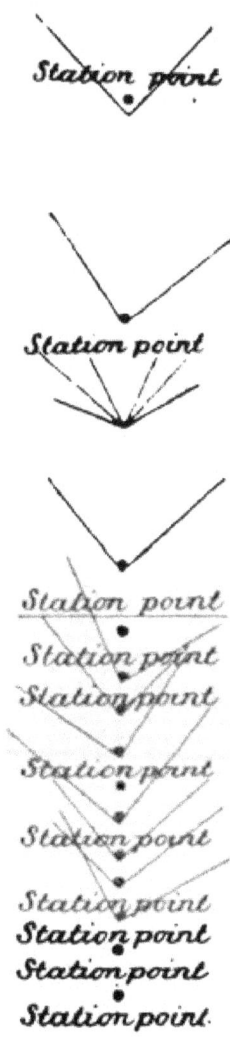

Station point

Station point

Station point
Station point
Station point
Station point
Station point
Station point
Station point
Station point

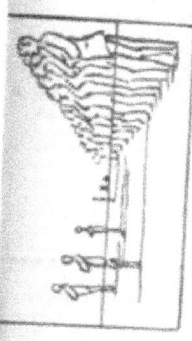

is perspective in clouds, in trees—indeed, the adaptation of it is endless, and unless the artist has some knowledge of its principles he cannot draw truthfully the humblest object. It is to be hoped, therefore, that the rules contained in this little pamphlet may be found helpful. They, at least, have the merit of being easy and true.

GENERAL REMARKS

ON

LINEAR PERSPECTIVE.

ADAPTED FROM THE FRENCH

OF

J. T. THIBAULT,

Membre de l'Institut, Professeur à l'Ecole Royale des Beaux Arts, &c.

Ars probat artificem.

LONDON :
WINSOR & NEWTON, Limited, 38, RATHBONE PLACE.

door to the station point, and laying that distance on the horizontal line. Then draw from the measurement on the measuring line B, by the dividing point to C, and that will give the desired width of the door, as by Example 18. The same rule applies to both doors.

The foregoing rules will be found to comprise all that is most needed in sketching from nature, whether for interior or outdoor work, and can be adapted to much that is found difficult without. For instance, there is perspective needed in giving the size of figures in a picture.

Take the height of a man to be eight heads high, place the figure the height you wish it to be in the foreground of the picture; a line taken from the top of the head and again at the feet, drawn to the point of sight, will give the size of the figure throughout the picture. There is perspective in clouds, in trees—indeed, the adaptation of it is endless, and unless the artist has some knowledge of its principles he cannot draw truthfully the humblest object. It is to be hoped, therefore, that the rules contained in this little pamphlet may be found helpful. They, at least, have the merit of being easy and true.

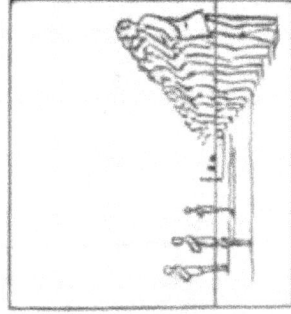

GEN

LINEA

ADAPT

Membre de l'Instit

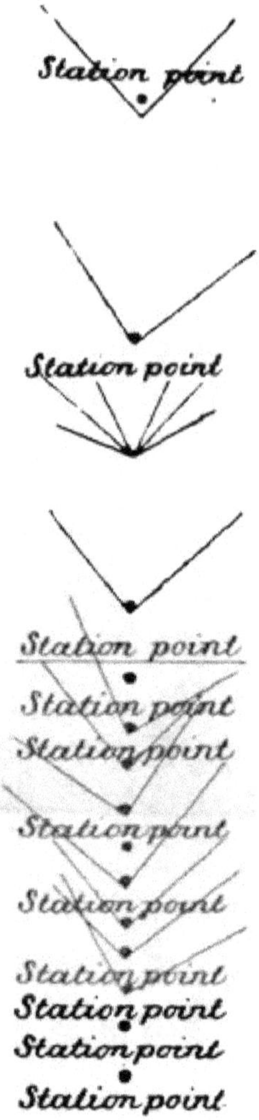

Station point

Station point

Station point
Station point
Station point
Station point
Station point
Station point
Station point
Station point
Station point

WINSOR & NE

GENERAL REMARKS

LINEAR PERSPECTIVE.

ADAPTED FROM THE FRENCH

OF

J. T. THIBAULT,

Membre de l'Institut, Professeur à l'Ecole Royale des Beaux Arts, &c.

Ars probat artificem.

WINSOR & NEWTON, Limited, 38, RATHBONE PLACE.

LINEAR PERSPECTIVE.[*]

THE THEORY OF PERSPECTIVE, ITS DEFINITIONS AND PRINCIPLES; OBSERVATIONS ON THE EFFECTS IN NATURE UPON WHICH THEY ARE DEPENDENT. —REMARKS ON THE POINT OF SIGHT AND ON THE PRINCIPAL POINT OF THE PICTURE; ALSO ON THE PRINCIPAL DISTANCE, ON THE HORIZONTAL LINE, VANISHING LINES AND POINTS, ETC.

According to geometry, Perspective consists in representing on a plane surface, of which the form and position are known, any objects as they would appear to an eye which should be placed at a given spot.

If we suppose that a straight line moves freely in any direction from a fixed point, and, without quitting this point, travels round the extremities of a given object, and that this line in its course intersects a plane surface on which it leaves the outline of the

* Linear Perspective requires no ground-plan, but is the application of a few simple problems in descriptive geometry. It is better suited for the general use of artists than the ground-plan method employed by architects and engineers. The preceding pages by Miss RUNCIMAN furnish the student with examples of Linear Perspective.—ED.

object that it has travelled round, this outline will be
a perspective projection of the object.

The eye being placed at a fixed point, the line from
it is a visual ray, the plane surface intersected is the
picture, and the outline made by the ray on this
picture is the perspective appearance of the object.

According to painters, Perspective is the art of
tracing on a picture all sorts of objects with sufficient
exactness for these painted objects to appear as if
they were real, and as if they were seen behind this
picture imagined as a transparent plane.

This last definition is incomplete; but it suffices for
the art of painting, which admits some licence in this
practice of Perspective. As we meet, in different
treatises on Perspective, with divers names and terms
which mean the same thing, we will, in order to
remove all difficulty, commence with a set of such
definitions as are essential.

We shall readily understand the theory of Perspective if we suppose that our eye is placed at a fixed spot,
and that a transparent plane is set up perpendicularly between us and the natural objects that we wish
to represent, in such a manner that we can see them
through this plane and trace them on the surface :
this tracing will be the exact perspective of the objects.
It is by following out the result of such an assumption
that means have been found to trace on a picture not
transparent the perspective representation of a natural

object, provided that its form, its dimensions, and the
space that it ought to occupy are known to us.

DEFINITIONS OF THE NAMES AND TERMS EMPLOYED IN PERSPECTIVE BY DIFFERENT AUTHORS.*

A *visual ray* is the straight line along which a
luminous point travels to arrive at our eye.

The *optical angle* is that which is formed at the eye
by the two rays which start from each extremity of
the object.

The *optical cone* is the collection of innumerable
rays starting from all the points of visible objects,
which are its base, and meeting at the centre of the
eye, which is its summit.

The *point of sight*, or point of the eye, is the summit of the optical cone.

The *principal* or central *ray*, the axis of this
optical cone, is the perpendicular dropped from the
eye to the picture.

The middle of the picture or *central point* is what
most authors have improperly called the point of sight,
or point of the eye ; this point is the section of the
principal ray on the picture,

The *picture*, or plan of projection, usually placed

* The first term that we shall quote in each definition will be that
which we shall make use of in the course of this book.

vertically in front of the spectator, is the limited surface on which one represents the object; and the *plane of the picture* is this same surface prolonged indefinitely in all directions.

The *principal distance*, or distance of the eye, is the direct interval between the eye of the spectator and the picture, traversed by the principal ray.

The *natural horizon* is that circular line which appears to separate the sky from the earth when no obstacle interferes with the whole extent of the view; the eye of the spectator being the centre of this horizon.

The horizon of the picture is the *horizontal line* which passes through the principal point. The principal vertical line, or *vertical line* of the picture, is a line which also passes through the principal point and which is perpendicular to the horizon.

Points of distance are points placed on the horizon, or on the vertical line of the picture, and which are removed on both sides from the principal point as far as the principal distance that they represent.

The *ground-plan* is the surface on which the objects are placed that are to be represented in the picture.

The *perspective plane* is that part of the picture which is comprised between its base and its horizon.

The *base of the picture* is the intersection of the plane of the picture with the ground-plan.

The term *natural object* is applied to everything

that we propose to represent, whether natural or artificial.

The terms *perspective elevation* and *projection* of the natural object are used for its representation in perspective in the picture.

Vanishing points are those at which retiring lines, parallel to each other, meet, or towards which they converge; for instance, the *principal point* is the vanishing point of all the lines at right angles to the plane of the picture; and the distance points placed on the horizontal line are the vanishing points of all the horizontal lines that make half a right angle (45°) with the plane of the picture. All the other vanishing points are called *accidental* ones: *super-horizontal* those that are above the horizontal line and *sub-horizontal* those that are below it.

Parallel surfaces or *lines* are those that are parallel to the plane of the picture.

Retiring surfaces or *lines* are those that are not parallel to the plane of the picture.

The *perspective width* of an object is its horizontal dimension when parallel to the plane of the picture; its *perspective height* being its vertical measurement under the same condition.

Depth in perspective is the measurement of a retiring surface calculated from the eye to the horizon; for example, the total depth of the perspective plan of a picture is the space which extends from its base to the horizon.

A *plain* or *geometrical scale* is a straight line parallel to the plane of the picture and divided into equal parts, which represent certain recognised measurements : it is usually placed below the picture.

A *retiring scale* is a straight line represented as being on the perspective plane of the picture and directed from its base to its horizon ; this scale is divided into .parts diminishing perspectively, which represent equal measurements.

REMARKS ON THE DIFFERENT APPEARANCES THAT THE SAME OBJECTS PRESENT TO OUR EYES, ACCORDING TO THE DISTANCE AT WHICH THEY ARE SEEN AND ACCORDING TO THEIR VARIED POSITIONS ; ON WHICH APPEARANCES THE PRINCIPLES AND RULES OF PERSPECTIVE ARE FOUNDED.

All objects seem to diminish in size in proportion to the distance they are removed from us.

Every object disappears at a greater or less distance according to its size : we presuppose that it is seen under a clear atmosphere, without considering the effect of mist, smoke, &c.

Parallel lines continued to a great distance appear to approach each other, and to meet in a point at their extremities if continued far enough : a long avenue of trees exemplifies this effect.

A horizontal plane at the level of the eye will appear

as a straight line, because we only see the extremity of the plane.

A horizontal surface placed below the level **of the** eye appears to rise as it recedes ; such is the effect of the sea or of a very extensive **plain,** which seem to rise towards the horizon.

A horizontal **surface placed above the level of the** eye seems to get lower as it recedes ; this **effect is** produced by the ceiling of a long gallery.

The same cause produces all these effects : that is to say, **the** apparent diminution in **the** size of the objects and of the distances between them in proportion as they are removed from us.

If a straight line, divided into equal parts, is seen in front, its divisions will always appear equal ; but if this line is seen obliquely, its equal divisions will appear unequal.

Lines actually parallel when seen **in** front always appear parallel in perspective.

The perspective of any plane figure, when parallel **to the** plane of the picture, is a figure resembling the original : thus a square, a circle, or a polygon, when parallel to the plane of the picture, do not change their form in perspective, but only their size according to their distance from the eye ; but when these figures are presented obliquely to our eyes they appear changed in form, the circle having the appearance of an oval, the square that of a trapezium, &c.

A straight line which is identical in direction with a visual ray only appears to the eye as a point.

A surface on which a visual ray can be laid down only appears to the eye as a line, because we only see its extremity, which is a line.

Lastly, a solid which only presents to view one of its sides appears as a simple surface.

REMARKS ON THE POINT OF SIGHT AND THE PRINCIPAL POINT.

In a picture we can only represent an object in a single position, an action or scene at a single instant, a view from a single point.

When we wish to draw or paint an object (or view) from Nature we usually place ourselves at a spot from which we can see easily, without being obliged to turn the head, the extremities of the object that we wish to represent, in such a way that the axis of the visual cone, or principal ray, is directed towards the middle of the object. It is the same in looking at and judging the effect of a picture ; for we naturally place ourselves opposite the middle of a picture, unless there is some special reason to the contrary, such, for instance, as an unpleasant reflection from a varnished surface in certain lights.

It follows from these remarks that all that is repre-

sented in a picture ought to be subordinated to a
single point of sight, and that the principal point
ought to be placed about the middle of the horizon of
the picture, unless there is some special reason to the
contrary. For instance, if to ornament the end of a
gallery we wished to paint several pictures by the
side of each other, with the idea of their being seen
from a certain given spot, and to produce the utmost
illusion possible, it might be that the principal point
would be found in neither one nor the other but
between the two; for it would be necessary that
these several pictures should be subordinated to a
single point.

The principal point is the vanishing point of all the
lines perpendicular to the surface of the picture.

When the position of a rectangular edifice is such
that one of its sides is parallel to the picture, which
may be easily recognised by noticing that the horizontal lines, such as cornices, window-sills, &c., on
this side appear parallel to each other, then these same
lines as they recede along one of the retiring sides of
this edifice will be examples of lines which are said to
be perpendicular to the picture: they should tend to
meet at the principal point, which is their vanishing
point.

Rectangular edifices may be so disposed that none
of their horizontal retiring lines tend to the principal
point. So that, though we have observed that it is

necessary for all the objects represented in a picture to be subordinated to a single point of sight, we must not conclude that all horizontal retiring lines ought to meet at the principal point.

REMARKS ON THE PRINCIPAL DISTANCE.

In the practice of Perspective the principal distance may be either given at first, taken as required, or indeed left undetermined. With reference to the distance, it is necessary in the first place to remark that we cannot see an object properly when we are either too near or too far off, and that the effect and success of a picture often depend upon a suitable choice of this distance.

The disagreeable effect that many perspective drawings produce is nearly always the result of choosing too short a distance at which to represent the objects drawn.

Natural objects can be seen from all points and under all aspects and yet appear always agreeable, because they are presented always directly to the sight whatever their position may be; or, rather, because we direct our attention to each one of the objects in turn. But the same objects represented on the surface of a picture have not this advantage : they cannot produce a satisfactory illusion if the distance at which to see and paint them properly has not been suitably selected.

The distance **will** be sufficient **if** when standing opposite the point of sight we can easily see at once all the limits of the picture.

All the objects represented in a picture ought to be subordinated to the same **distance,** and the distance may be regulated by a given object. In **practice,** painters hardly ever determine with **precision the** principal distance ; but when they have sketched on their picture some symmetrical object of **which their** taste approves the appearance, they have unconsciously determined this distance, which is throughout the rest of the design subordinated to this first object, and very often there is no occasion to fix it absolutely. Sometimes, however, it is necessary to find it in order to complete the work which may have been commenced without it.

ESSENTIAL REMARKS.

When, in order to look at a picture which has been drawn according to the rules of perspective, one is placed **at** its point of sight—that is to say, at the distance selected as suitable by the painter—this picture, properly painted, ought to produce the utmost illusion possible.

If to inspect this same picture one approaches closer, so as to be between its point of sight and its surface, the objects represented will still preserve their forms

agreeably ; only this surface, of which one will not be
so easily able to see the whole extent, will seem to
retire from the eye. But if, on the contrary, one
places oneself further than the point of view chosen
by the artist, the objects represented will appear more
or less distorted. It is especially in pictures which
represent architecture, or in symmetrical objects, that
these effects will assert themselves most noticeably.

It is therefore preferable that the principal distance
should be made rather greater than less, in order that
the spectator of the picture should rather be disposed
to place himself too near than too far off ; so that, in
all the cases where we wish to settle the point of
distance at first, it will be advisable to place it at the
most distant spot at which the picture can be seen
satisfactorily.

Objects put into perspective according to the rules
but at too short a distance are not agreeable to the
eye. We can prove this statement by referring to the
examples engraved in many well-written treatises on
the subject, in which the points of distance have been
placed at the sides of the picture in order to render
the instructions more clear and intelligible. These
figures, occurring in excellent books, have caused
many people to imagine that scientific perspective is
at fault, because such representations of objects
appear unmistakeably distorted.

All the authors who have pretended to give rules

for establishing the principal distance have only advanced private opinions on the subject, for there does not exist any general rule.

In several treatises on Perspective we find rules for determining the principal distance : some fix it at the angle comprised in the quarter of a circle, others at the angle comprised in the sixth part, while again others make it equal to the largest dimension of the picture. Without prejudging these rules, we are going to instance those of the celebrated painters and architects who have combined example and precept.

Leonardo da Vinci says that, to design an object from Nature, it is necessary to be removed from that object at a distance equal to three times its height ; elsewhere he advises making the principal distance equal to double the size of the picture. To reconcile these two passages of Leonardo, which appear contradictory, it must be noticed that the object of which he speaks at first—for instance, a human figure—ought not to occupy the whole surface of the picture on which it is represented, and that thus the principal distance may be at the same time three times the height of the figure and double the size of the picture.

Balthazar Perruzzi and, after him, Sebastian Serlio, his pupil, have also established the distance on the dimension of the picture, and have made it equal to one and a half times the measurement of its base.

Ignazio Danti, in his commentaries on the Perspective of Vignola, says that the pupil of the eye can admit an angle slightly larger than the sixth part of a circle ; but that, as a picture ought to be seen at a glance and without moving the head, this angle would produce too short a distance : that we must therefore suppose the angle more acute, in order that the distance may be greater, and that the extremities of the visual pyramid may be better seen ; that he himself decided to take for *distance* the height of a triangle of which the base is equal to two-thirds of this height, and even to half in certain cases. He found that by this means the two great inconveniences which result from too short a distance are avoided : the one is that horizontal surfaces appear to slope upwards too suddenly as they retire, and the horizontal eaves of buildings to slope downwards too much ; the other is that a marked-out square is apt to appear deeper than it is wide.

There is a letter extant of Nicholas Poussin in which he refers to his selection of the point of distance for the pictures that he painted to adorn the grand gallery of the Louvre. " It must be observed," he writes, "that the wainscot of the gallery is twenty-one feet high and twenty-four feet long from one window to another ; the width of the gallery, which determines the distance for viewing the wall-space, is also twenty-four feet ; the central panel of the wain-

scot is twelve feet long by nine feet high ; so that the
width of the gallery gives a distance suitably propor-
tioned for seeing at a glance a picture which should
fit the panel." It will be seen by these **measurements** that the *distance* is equal to twice the **base of**
the picture ; the book on Perspective by Desargue,
which A. Bosse sent to Poussin, at Rome, also con-
firms this choice. But Poussin did not confine himself exclusively to this distance.

Modern oculists affirm that, in order to see at once
easily and clearly all the extremities of an object, the
eye must be removed from that object at a distance at
least equal to double its greatest dimension. However, it is to be remarked that in several of the most
celebrated pictures (among others in Raphael's School
of Athens) the principal distance is only about that of
the base ; but we believe it will never be found to be
less than the base or width of the picture.

Lastly, we will observe that architects, who usually
employ a ground-plan and geometrical elevation of
a building in order to put it into perspective, first
determine the point of view, which settles at the same
time the principal distance ; but that painters, as we
have already pointed out, only indicate this distance
by its effects, unless they should **have** some special
reasons to determine it.

REMARKS ON THE NATURAL HORIZON AND ON THE HORIZON OF THE PICTURE.

The natural horizon is a circular line; but this line, being on a plane at the level of the eye (which is at its centre), appears straight. At a glance, and without turning the head, one can only see a part of the horizon, which invariably appears at the level of the eye of the spectator, wherever he may be placed.

The character of the country, whether mountainous or not, in which painters dwell, often influences their taste in the determining whereabouts in their pictures the horizon should be placed. Thus it may be noticed that in the pictures of the Italian school the horizons are usually very high, while on the contrary they are very low in the pictures of the Dutch and Flemish schools.

The horizon of a picture is the first thing that should be decided on, as all the objects in the picture must be subordinated to this one horizon.

When one is sketching a landscape from Nature the horizon is invariably fixed. If the view is bounded by the sea, the horizon is visible; if not, one must find it, which is not difficult: for, if the painter imagines a line on the level of his eye, and supposes this line to reach to a point on some visible object, this point will give him the height of the horizon with sufficient exactness for the purposes of his picture.

We would here remark that a picture placed vertically in a suitable position will not produce all its effect unless its horizon is at the height of the spectator's eye or—still better—rather below it. It is also the advice of Poussin ; who, in the postscript of a letter written from Rome to M. de Chanteloup, to announce the sending to him of one of his pictures, adds, " Before showing it, it would be advisable to frame it, and it ought to be placed rather below than above the eye."

We will add, lastly, that a picture put in an elevated position will only produce all the illusion possible when it is tilted forward in such a manner that a ray from the eye of the spectator, placed at a suitable distance, arrives perpendicularly to the horizon of the picture.

There does not exist any certain rule for fixing the height of the horizon when composing a picture ; it depends upon the taste of the painter, his choice of subject, and the extent of the view to be represented.

Leonardo da Vinci says that he who wishes to draw a human figure from Nature ought to place himself so that the eye of his model should be on a level with his own ; but this is only with reference to portraiture, and is, after all, but an individual opinion.

In historical pictures and other works of imagina-
tion the painter is at liberty to place the horizon at
three different heights relatively to the human figures
that he wishes to represent : either on a level with
the eyes of these figures, or above that level, or below
it. In the first case the painter is supposed to be
standing or sitting on the same ground as his models ;
in the second case he is supposed to be on higher
ground ; and in the third case on lower.

These remarks, the importance of which will appear
later on, teach us to judge at a glance whether the
human figures in a picture which was supposed to be
on level ground, but at different distances, are
designed correctly in perspective ; they also teach us
to put figures into pictures with the diminished height
that they should each have according to their
respective distances from the plane of the picture.

REMARKS ON THE VANISHING POINTS.

Since parallel retiring lines, prolonged to a very
great distance, appear to approach each other and
to meet at last in a single point, if we imagine a
visual ray directed to this point, this ray will then be
parallel to these lines; and, conversely, if lines appear
to meet at a point with a visual ray, these lines will
then be parallel to this ray.

In effect, if with the eye fixed in one spot we
trace on a transparent vertical plane, such as a window, the parallel **retiring lines seen** through it, we
shall see that the **lines thus traced** will meet at the
point indicated by **the track of the** visual ray on the
window parallel to the **lines referred to.**

It follows from this, that, in order to find in a picture the vanishing point of as many original parallel
lines as one wishes to represent, it will be sufficient
to direct a ray from the eye parallel to these lines.
The section of this ray on the surface of the picture
will be the point of sight to which the perspective
appearances of these parallels will tend.

This is the general principle of the vanishing points
which Guido Ubaldo first published in his book on
Perspective printed in 1600 ; but he only applied this
principle to the parallel lines on the horizontal and
vertical planes ; it has since been applied to parallel
lines on all the inclined planes, whatever their position.
Thus, if we suppose the plane of the picture infinitely
extended, the appearance of all the parallel lines which
are at any inclination to this plane will have a vanishing
point on it. But the appearance of all those lines
which are at the same time parallel to each other and
to the plane of the picture cannot have a vanishing
point on this plane. Since they never reached it,
they do not meet, and remain always parallel in the
perspective view. Vanishing points are very useful

in the practice of Perspective, for not only do they shorten the operations but they give them more precision.

Lastly, it must be observed that the vanishing points are often found to be beyond the limits of the picture ; they are then inaccessible, or considered as such, and must be supplied. We have recourse to geometry, which gives several methods of obtaining them.

REMARKS ON THE GEOMETRICAL AND PERSPECTIVE
SCALES : THAT IS TO SAY, PLAIN AND DIMINISHING
SCALES.

Plain scales serve to determine questions of height and width in perspective representations : that is to say, the dimensions of all the objects on the planes of surfaces parallel to the plane of the picture.

Diminishing scales serve to determine questions of depth in perspective : that is to say, the dimensions of objects on planes which retire from the base of the picture towards its horizon.

All the objects which enter into the composition of a picture can mutually serve to establish their relative proportions ; but the most natural standard of measurement, the oldest and at all times the most familiar to the painter, is the stature of the human figure. Pythagoras says that " man is the measure

of all things, because everything can be compared to
him ; "and another ancient writer, in describing the
lighthouse of Alexandria says "that its height was
three hundred cubits, **or one hundred** statures ;"
meaning by this word the **average height** of a man.
We still use the expression, **and say that a man is**
of high, average, or low stature.

We employ this standard of **measurement,** which,
being only relative and able **to** be established arbi-
trarily, will serve for scale ; especially for historical
and genre painters, who ordinarily begin by determining on their canvas the height of one of the figures,
and who afterwards design **all** the other objects in
proportion with this figure. **To use** this standard
measurement of stature **as a scale we can** divide it
into an equal number of parts. **It is in this** way
that Tomaso Lauretti, a Sicilian painter, made a
graduated scale, hitherto unknown : he divided the
stature into eight heads, and subdivided the head
into four equal parts ; he put these measurements
into perspective, and formed squares, which by their
gradual diminution not only gave him the height of a
human figure, but also the measurement of each part
of this figure at all the planes of his picture.

All the objects, in painting, appear large or small
according to their relations with any human figure
that may be in the picture : it is doubtless by this
comparison that Timanthes made the Greeks admire

the gigantic stature of a sleeping Cyclops that he had
painted in a picture, along with three little Satyrs
who measured, with their thyrsi, the great toe of the
sleeper.

COMMON FAULTS IN PERSPECTIVE.

The most noticeable faults that occur in pictures,
and which strike the eye unpleasantly, are caused,
firstly, by the distance being badly chosen (generally
too short); and, secondly from the horizon being
undetermined or badly placed with reference to the
objects represented, or from those objects being badly
placed with regard to the horizon. We have already
observed that the spectator is placed too near an
object to draw it properly when he cannot easily see
its whole extent at a glance, and is obliged to turn
his head to one side and the other in order to see its
extremities. A faithful representation—that is to say,
the exact perspective appearance—of an object taken
in this manner appears defective : its right angles
appear acute, its horizontal planes above and below
the eye seem to rise or descend too rapidly, its
retiring sides seem too deep, and the whole appears
distorted and disagreeable. Thus it often happens
that in spite of correct drawing from Nature a painting is disfigured through ignorance, not of the rules,
but of the principles of perspective. That a suffi-

ciently long distance should be chosen is the condition
of all others requisite **for producing** an agreeable
perspective representation. If this condition is not
fulfilled—and we cannot too often repeat the remark—
the picture will offend the eye ; and **the more truth-**
fully the view is rendered the **more disagreeable will**
be its effect.

In the case of a panorama, the perspective is not
controlled by any principal vanishing point, because
the visual rays are perpendicular to its cylindrical
concave surface. Experience has even taught us that
it is not absolutely necessary to **be at** the centre of
the panorama to enjoy its effect.

We have already observed that it is necessary that
all the objects represented in a picture should be
controlled by its horizon ; and that when a painter
has designed any figures the horizon of the picture is
determined, and that this horizon ought to regulate
all the other objects which enter into the composition.
Portraits are frequently painted with the horizon
about the height of the eye, showing that the painter
and his sitter were on a level ; and yet the backgrounds
will be controlled by a totally different horizon. The
result is unsatisfactory to most spectators, who see
that there is something wrong but cannot tell what it
is that interferes with the proper unity of effect.

We will now allude to a fault of perspective caused
by the horizon not having been determined in the

picture. The picture referred to represented a landscape in which were painted several figures on a level road at different depths in the picture. These figures had no relative proportion to each other : those far in the picture, much too small, seemed to be pygmies compared with those in the foreground of the picture ; for in supposing the horizon determined by the near figures, those far in would have had a quarter of a stature in height. One could not suppose that the ground on which the figures were placed became lower as it retired, because it bordered a lake, the horizontal surface of which followed that of the ground at a slightly lower level.

We will also allude to another error in perspective, doubtless resulting from the carelessness of the artist, since the horizon was represented in the picture. A human figure was placed on the summit of an edifice which stood well above the horizon, but was so represented that one saw at once up under the feet of the figure and down on to the shoulders.

Besides the faults we have pointed out, the most common errors in perspective occur, firstly, when all the objects which compose a picture (as figures, buildings, landscapes, &c.) have been designed from different distances—that is to say, are not taken from the same point of view ; secondly, when all the objects represented in the picture are not regulated by the same horizon ; thirdly, when the retiring lines

that the painter has intended to make appear parallel
to each other, do not tend to the same vanishing
point ; and, fourthly, when the buildings are not
represented in their proper proportion to the human
figures in the picture. We may remark that, in the
last case, if it should happen that there are figures in
the foreground and buildings further back, and that
the buildings are too small relatively to the figures,
this error of proportion may be obviated by indicating
a change of level between the surface where the figures
are placed and that on which the buildings stand.   In
other words, we suppose the figures to be standing
on a kind of terrace, the height of which (above the
ground on which the buildings are) cannot be calculated because its base is not seen, but is always
imagined to be such as to justify the relative proportions given to the figures and the buildings.   Thus, by
changing the appearance of height of the ground on
which objects rest, we can make these objects appear
greater or smaller in perspective without augmenting
or diminishing their measured height in the picture.

ARTISTIC LICENCES IN PERSPECTIVE.

If we suppose that a picture, of which the perspective
is correctly drawn according to the rules of this art,
will only be seen from the point chosen by the artist—
that is to say, from the point of view to which all the

objects are conformed—then the most trifling licences
cannot be allowed in such a work ; not only would
they be useless, but they would mar the effect and the
illusion **produced.** Rigorous precision is absolutely
required.

But a picture of large size designed to decorate a
large hall or gallery would be seen at the same time
by a considerable number of spectators, while it could
only be seen from its **true** point by one person at a
time ; and, in order that everybody should see it from
this **point, it would be necessary that each** person
should place himself there in turn, which would be
impracticable, especially if there was a crowd of
spectators. It is not in this way that very large and
celebrated pictures are regarded. The spectators, far
from remaining at the same spot where they first placed
themselves in order to see the general effect, move
about to the right and then to the left for the purpose
of examining necessarily all the details that compose
the work. But let us suppose that this picture **has**
been outlined with geometrical precision, that all the
objects which compose it are regulated by a single
point of view, and that their perspective projection is
rigorously correct ; then this is the result which will
be produced : the spectator removed from the point
of view and placed opposite either of the ends of the
picture, will see the objects in front of him more or less
distorted ; for it may happen that, in consequence of

the correct application of the rules of perspective, a human head may appear as wide as it is high, which would be monstrous and ridiculous.

We believe, then, that a painter ought not always to subject himself to the strict laws of perspective ; that it is allowable to take certain licences ; that he ought always to draw his subjects in such a manner that they will be agreeable to the eye from whatever place they are looked at. We do not even think that he can do otherwise ; for all the great masters, ancient and modern, have followed and still follow this method. Thus, according to the usage of the best artists, the whole effect of a large picture ought to be submitted to the laws of perspective, and the objects which compose it ought to be considered relatively to each other, following the rules of this art ; but in order to draw each object in detail, especially human figures, one may and even ought to take some licences, to abandon sometimes the absolute precision of geometry, and to content oneself with such an approximation as good taste can approve. The licences of which we are speaking may have a sort of law which is not rigorous, but of which the eye may be regarded as the final judge.

It is in the representation of buildings and other rectangular objects that the defects of perspective are most apparent.

We will now call attention to several particular

cases which authorize or permit the use of some licences in the practice of perspective.

According to the rules of perspective, the principal point ought to be placed in the middle of its horizon; but the painters have not always followed this rule, as, for instance, Poussin in his picture of the lame man cured by the Apostles.

When the principal point is removed considerably from the centre of the picture, and a rectangular edifice presents two of its sides, the one parallel and the other perpendicular to the plane of the picture, it happens sometimes that the horizontal lines (which form the eaves, cornices, &c.) of the side parallel to the plane of the picture seem to incline in an unnatural manner, and to rise towards the side of the picture the furthest off from the principal point; then it is necessary to allow a licence, by inclining slightly the horizontal lines and lowering them from the same side till the eye judges them to be parallel to the horizon. A very slight inclination is sufficient to make them produce this effect.

The perspective projection of a sphere is a circle that can be drawn by a compass when its centre is in the visual ray perpendicular to the plane of the picture—that is to say, at the principal point; but when the centre of this sphere is more or less removed from this point, its perspective appearance is that of an ellipse more or less elongated. A very simple experiment will illustrate, **so to** speak, the **sceno-**graphic projection of a sphere on a plane.

If we suspend a sphere between a bright light and a wall, we shall see that the shadow of this sphere will be circular as long as its centre is in the perpendicular ray transmitted from **the** centre **of** the light on to the wall; but if the sphere is removed more or less from the perpendicular ray, we shall see that the shadow thrown on to the wall will **be** elliptical, and more or less elongated, according as the projection is cast more or less obliquely. **A** similar experiment may be made with sunlight **by** suspending a sphere and changing the position of the plane surface on which the shadow is cast.

The spheres that Raphael **has** painted **in** his "School of Athens" are placed at the extreme side of the picture, towards the right. If they were exactly in perspective, their elliptical appearance, considerably elongated, would make an odd contrast to their actual form, which would be the more noticeable as the figures which carry them are not themselves very rigorously in perspective; so Raphael took the liberty of describing these spheres with the compass.

Artistic licences may be **taken** in all kinds of painting. For instance, when one draws from Nature **an** exterior or interior view of a building, and one finds oneself with a wall at one's back, or some other obstacle which prevents one from getting far enough

away from the object that one wishes to represent, in
order to show it under its most favourable aspect it
is necessary to make the spectator believe that the
wall or other obstacle did not exist, and that one was
quite at liberty as to the spot one should select as
the point of view, and so to place oneself where one
liked. There is no fear but that the spectator will
forgive the artist this licence, or rather this false
statement, even if he should know it to be untrue ;
since it will have been the means of rendering the
picture more agreeable, and of increasing his own
pleasure in looking at it.

We may say, in conclusion, that no one will be
shocked at any licence in perspective that a painter
may have taken when it neither offends his eye nor
his reason, and while it tends in the direction of
grace and beauty.

THE END.

Printed by
SHEPPARD & ST. JOHN, 0, St. Bride Street, Ludgate Circus, London, E.C.

WINSOR & NEWTON.

CATALOGUE

OF

COLOURS & MATERIALS

FOR

OIL COLOUR PAINTING,

ETC., ETC.

TRADE MARK.

Ars probat artificem.

WINSOR & NEWTON, Limited,

Manufacturing Artists' Colourmen by Special Appointment to
HER MAJESTY,

And Their Royal Highnesses the Prince and Princess of Wales.

37, 38, 39 & 40, RATHBONE PLACE, LONDON, W.

1886.

PRIZE MEDAL

OF THE

GREAT EXHIBITION of 1851,

AWARDED TO

WINSOR & NEWTON,

(Class II.—Chemistry), for Artists' Colours.

This was a competitive Exhibition. Messrs. WINSOR & NEWTON carried off the only Medal that was awarded to the competitors (English and Foreign) for Artists' Colours.

PRIZE MEDAL

OF THE

INTERNATIONAL EXHIBITION of 1862,

AWARDED TO

WINSOR & NEWTON,

(Class II.—Chemistry. Section A. No. 627).

The award of a Prize Medal to Messrs. WINSOR & NEWTON, for their UNEQUALLED display of fine and costly Pigments, was accompanied by the following remarks from the Jurors, viz. :

"For a magnificent display of Artists' Colours, AND FOR THEIR ENDEAVOURS TO SUBSTITUTE PERMANENT COLOURS FOR THE MORE FUGITIVE PIGMENTS USED BY ARTISTS."

FINELY PREPARED OIL COLOURS.

WINSOR & NEWTON have long paid special attention to the production and preparation of their Artists' Oil Colours, which have attained their present high reputation by possessing characteristic qualities established by every variety of conclusive test.

The Pigments used are of the highest and purest quality.

At the "North London Colour Works," WINSOR and NEWTON, Limited, now possess every facility and appliance, for the production of manufactured colours, and for testing and purifying natural ones.

Grinding Artists' Colours by machinery was first commenced by WINSOR & NEWTON in 1844, special apparatus being invented by them for the purpose. Since that period still further improvements have been made; and at present there exists no machinery which for power and precision, combined with great cleanliness in working, can at all compare with that invented, perfected, and now used by them for grinding Artists' Oil Colours.

There are no mediums or admixtures in the preparation of these Colours. Consequently they keep fresh and pure, and ready for use.

Briefly, it may be stated, that the best and purest pigments, most thoroughly ground in unadulterated Oil, form the ingredients of their Artists' Oil Colours, causing them to take the foremost rank, and to be the colours generally used, both at home and abroad.

WINSOR & NEWTON'S

FINELY PREPARED OIL COLOURS,

IN COLLAPSIBLE TUBES.

(Sizes of the Tubes).

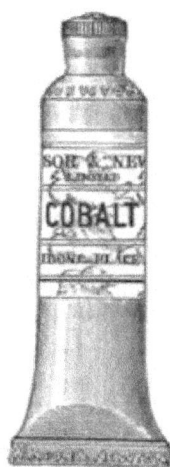

2-INCH TUBE.

2-INCH TUBE

4-INCH TUBE.

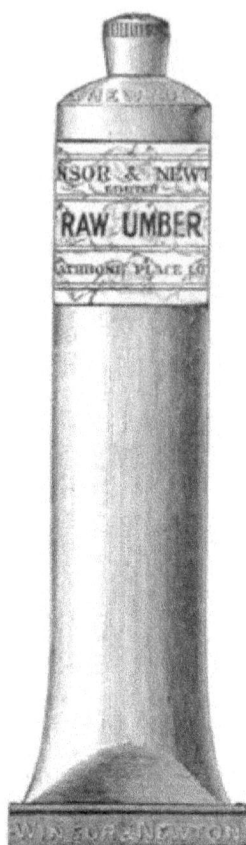

DOUBLE TUBE.

TREBLE TUBE.

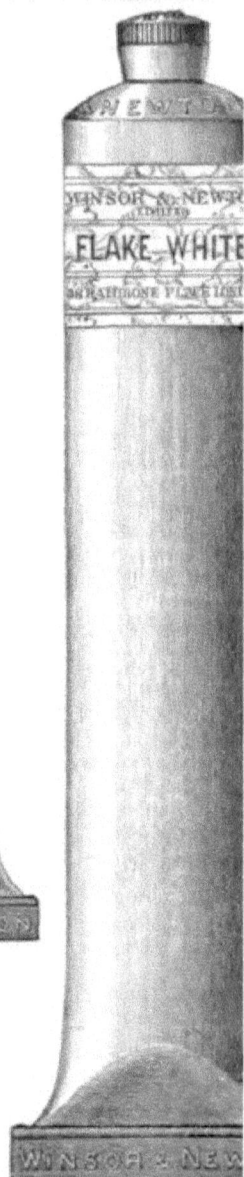

QUADRUPLE TUBE.

(Particulars and Prices follow on the next two Pages.)

WINSOR & NEWTON'S
FINELY PREPARED OIL COLOURS,
IN COLLAPSIBLE TUBES.

(See Illustrations on the two previous pages.)

4d. EACH.

Antwerp Blue	King's Yellow
Asphaltum (thick)	Lamp Black
Bitumen	Light Red
Black Lead	Magenta
Blue Black	Mauve
Bone Brown	Medium
Brown Ochre	Megilp
Brown Pink	Mummy
Burnt Roman Ochre	Naples Yellow, French
Burnt Sienna	Naples Yellow
Burnt Umber	Neutral Tint
Caledonian Brown	New Blue
Cappah Brown	Nottingham White
Cassel Earth	Olive Lake
Chinese Blue	Orpiment
Chrome Green, No. 1	Oxford Ochre
Chrome Green, No. 2	Payne's Grey
Chrome Green, No. 3	Permanent Blue
Chrome Lemon	Permanent White
Chrome Yellow	Permanent Yellow
Chrome, Deep	Prussian Blue
Chrome Orange	Prussian Brown
Chrome Red	Purple Lake
Cinnabar Green, Light	Pyne's Megilp
Cinnabar Green, Middle	Raw Sienna
Cinnabar Green, Deep	Raw Umber
Cologne Earth	Roman Ochre
Cool Roman Ochre	Sap Green
Copal Megilp	Scarlet Lake
Cork Black	Silver White
Cremnitz White	Sugar of Lead
Crimson Lake	Terra Rosa
Emerald Green	Terre Verte
Flake White	Transparent Gold Ochre
Gamboge	Vandyke Brown
Indian Lake	Venetian Red
Indian Red	Verdigris
Indigo	Verona Brown
Italian Pink	Yellow Lake
Ivory Black	Yellow Ochre
Jaune Brillant	Zinc White

All Colours can be had in Double, Treble, and Quadruple Tubes.

Winsor & Newton's Oil Colours in Tubes.—Continued.

(All Colours in this page are in Two-inch Tubes.)

6d. EACH.

Brown Madder	Geranium Lake
Burnt Lake	Sepia
Cerulean Blue	Vermilion
Chinese Vermilion	

1s. EACH.

Carmine, No. 2	Mars Yellow
Citron Yellow	Mineral Grey
Cobalt Blue	Orange Vermilion
Extract of Vermilion	Oxide of Chromium
French Ultramarine	Ditto, Transparent
French Veronese Green	Pink Madder
Lemon Yellow, Pale	Rembrandt's Madder
Lemon Yellow	Rose Madder
Madder Lake	Rubens' Madder
Malachite Green	Scarlet Vermilion
Mars Brown	Strontian Yellow
Mars Red	Viridian
Mars Violet	

1s. 6d. EACH.

Brilliant Ultramarine	Field's Orange **Vermilion**
(or Factitious Ultramarine)	Indian Yellow
Burnt Carmine	Madder Carmine
Cadmium Yellow	Mars Orange
Cadmium Yellow, Pale	Orient Yellow
Cadmium Orange	Purple Madder
Carmine (Finest)	Scarlet Madder
Crimson Madder	Violet Carmine
Extra Malachite Green	Yellow Carmine

2s. 6d. EACH.

Aureolin	Ultramarine Ash

4s. EACH.

Extra Madder Carmine	Extra Purple Madder

Genuine Ultramarine.

Medium strength, 10s. 6d. each.	Full strength 21s. each.

All Colours can be had in Double, Treble and Quadruple Tubes.

WINSOR & NEWTON'S
VARNISHES, OILS AND MEDIUMS.

	Round or Flat Glass Bottles. Each.	¼ Pints in Stone Bottles. Each.	½ Pints in Stone Bottles. Each.	Pints in Stone Bottles. Each.
	s. *d.*	*s.* *d.*	*s.* *d.*	*s.* *d.*
*Picture Mastic Varnish, for varnishing	1 6	3 0	5 6	10 0
*Mastic Varnish, for Megilp (double strength)	2 0	3 9	7 0	13 6
Amber Varnish, Dark...	1 6	3 0	5 6	10 0
Amber Varnish, Light .	2 0	3 9	7 0	13 6
*Picture Copal Varnish .	1 0	1 9	3 0	6 0
*Oil Copal Varnish ...	1 0	1 9	3 0	6 0
*White Spirit Varnish...	1 0	1 9	3 0	6 0
*Brown ditto ...	1 0	1 9	3 0	6 0
Crystal or Map Varnish	0 9	1 3	2 3	4 6
Japan Gold Size ...	0 8	1 0	2 0	3 9
Fat Oil	0 9	1 3	2 3	4 6
Nut Oil	0 6	1 0	1 6	3 0
Poppy Oil	0 6	1 0	1 6	3 0
Pale Drying Oil ...	0 6	0 10	1 3	2 3
Strong Drying Oil ...	0 6	0 10	1 3	2 3
Purified Linseed Oil ...	0 6	0 10	1 3	2 0
Spirits of Turpentine ...	0 5	0 7	1 0	1 6

* *These are also supplied in Half Bottles.*

	Bottles. Each.
	s. *d.*
Bessell's Medium for painting on silk, in water colours	1 6
Burrow's Keramic Medium for painting on china	1 6
Siccatif de Harlem (Duroziez's), for oil painting	1 3
Ditto large size bottles	2 6
Siccatif Courtray, for oil painting	0 9
Soehnee Varnish, for oil painting	1 0
Ditto large size bottles	2 0
Ditto for Water Colours	1 0
Adolfi Medium for painting on silk or satin, in oil colours	1 6
Ditto large size bottles	3 0
Carl Haag's Fixative for water-colour drawings ...	2 0
Turck's Florentine Medium for painting with Oil Colours on Tapestry, Satin, and Textile Fabrics	1 0
Turck's Mirrorine for painting with Oil Colours on Glass, China, and Terra Cotta...	1 0
Glassium Medium for Oil Painting	1 6

PALETTES.

SPANISH MAHOGANY AND SATIN WOOD.

 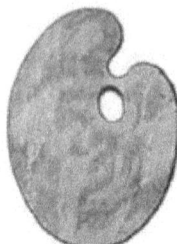 

No. 1 Shape.   No. 2 Shape.   No. 3 Shape.

SPANISH MAHOGANY.			s.	d.	SATIN WOOD.			s.	d.
8 inch	...	each	1	3	8 inch	...	each	2	6
9 ,,	...	,,	1	6	9 ,,	...	,,	2	9
10 ,,	...	,,	1	9	10 ,,	...	,,	3	0
11 ,,	...	,,	2	0	11 ,,	...	,,	3	3
12 ,,	...	,,	2	6	12 ,,	...	,,	4	0
13 ,,	...	,,	3	0	13 ,,	...	,,	4	6
14 ,,	...	,,	3	3	14 ,,	...	,,	5	0
15 ,,	...	,,	3	9	15 ,,	...	,,	5	6
16 ,,	...	,,	4	0	16 ,,	...	,,	6	0
17 ,,	...	,,	4	3	17 ,,	...	,,	6	9
18 ,,	...	,,	4	6	18 ,,	...	,,	7	6
12 ,, Folding palettes ..			3	9	12 ,, Folding palettes ..			5	6

No. 1 Shape is sent unless otherwise ordered.

Sycamore or White Wood Palettes are supplied at the same prices as Mahogany.

MAHL STICKS.

							s.	d.
Bamboo Mahl Sticks	...	...	...	...	...	each	0	6
Jointed Polished Bamboo Mahl Stick, in two pieces with Brass Joint ...					...	,,	2	9
Ditto, in three	,,	two Brass Joints		...	...	,,	3	0
,, in four	,,	three ,,		...	...	,,	4	0
,, in five	,,	four ,,		...	...	,,	4	6
Telescope Pocket Bamboo Mahl Sticks			...	..	,,		4	0
,, ,, Metal ,,			...	...	,,		4	0

WINSOR & NEWTON'S

JAPANNED TIN BOXES for OIL PAINTING
FITTED WITH COLOURS AND MATERIALS.

Winsor & Newton, Limited, have re-designed and improved most
of their Oil Colour Tube Boxes. The range is extensive, and may
be said to meet every requirement. These Boxes are convenient,
portable, and of the best Material and Workmanship.

PUPIL'S BOX.

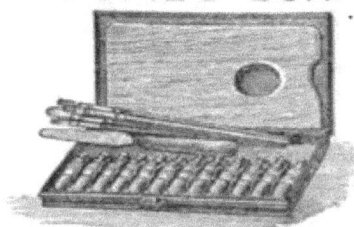

Price 6s.—fitted complete.   (Empty Box, with Mahogany Palette,
2s. 3d.)

Pupil's Box : Size 7¾ inches by 3¾, 1 inch deep, containing twelve
colours in 2-inch tubes, four Hog-hair Brushes, Mahogany Palette
and Palette Knife.

POCKET BOX.

Price 10s.—fitted complete.   (Empty Box, with Mahogany Palette,
3s. 6d.)

Pocket Box : Size 9¼ inches by 4¼, 1 inch deep, containing
twelve Colours, six Hog-hair Brushes, Mahogany Palette and
Palette Knife.

TOURIST'S BOX.

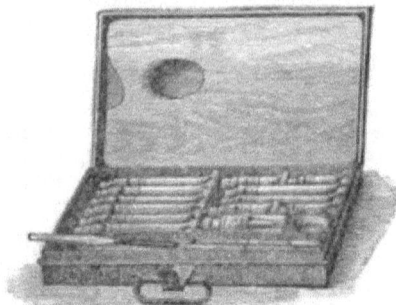

Price 12s. 6d.—fitted complete. (Empty Box, with Dipper, Bottle of Oil and Mahogany Palette, 6s. 6d.)

TOURIST'S BOX: Size, 9¼ inches by 6, 1¼ inch deep, containing twelve Colours, Brushes, Palette Knife, Oil, Dipper and Mahogany Palette.

STUDENT'S BOX.
WITH FLAP.

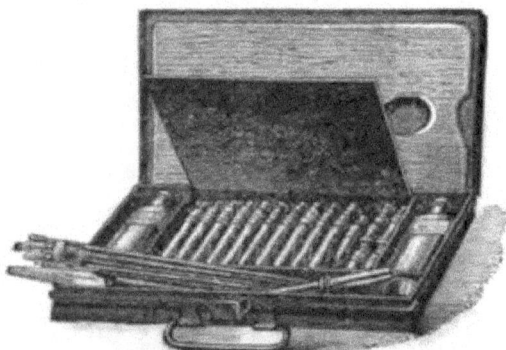

Price £1 1s.—fitted complete. (Empty Box, with Dipper, 7s. 6d.)

STUDENT'S BOX: Size 13¼ inches by 6½, 1½ inch deep: containing fifteen Colours, Sable and Hog-hair Brushes, Badger Softener, Chalk, Portcrayon, Dipper, Palette Knife, Oil, Turpentine, and Mahogany Palette.

COMPANION BOX.
WITH FLAP.

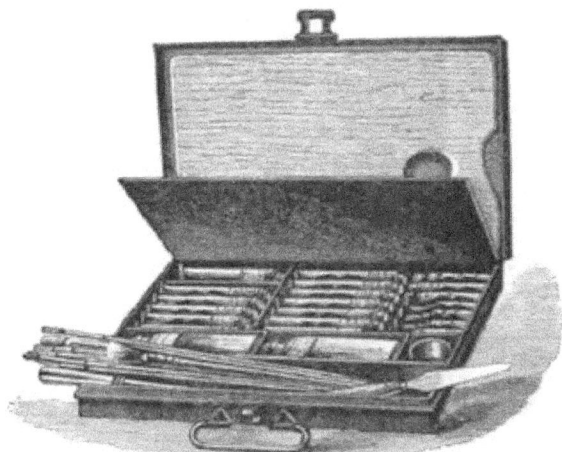

PORTABLE BOX.

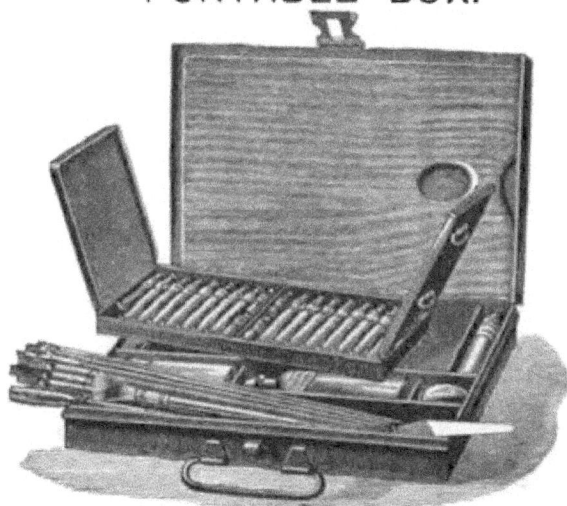

(For Prices and Particulars see page 17.)

DOUBLE PORTABLE BOX.

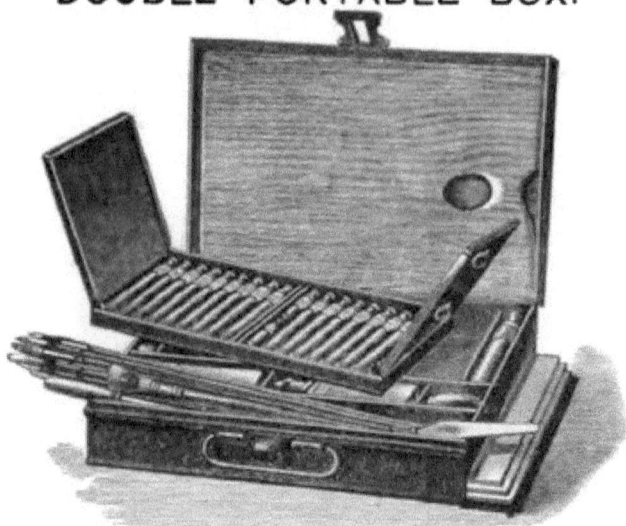

ACADEMY BOX.

(For Prices and Particulars see page 17.)

1.

2.

STUDIO BOX, No. 3.

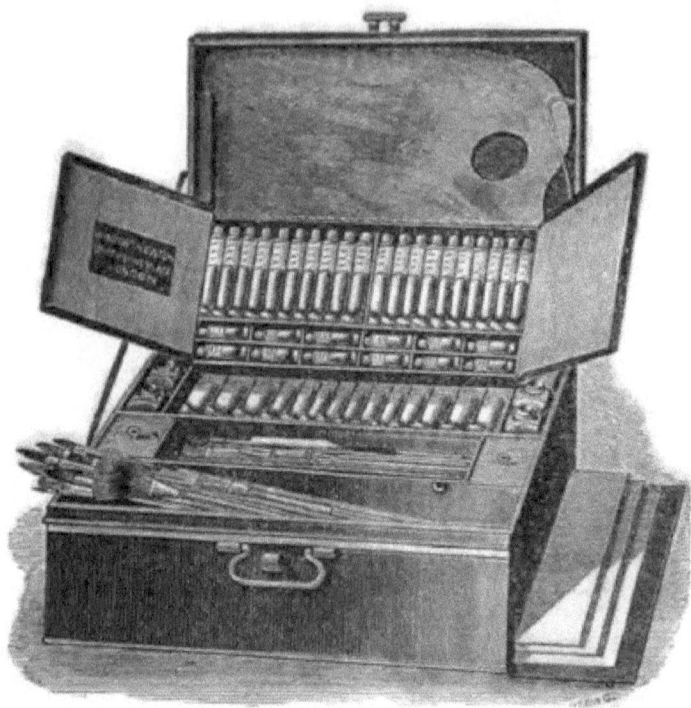

For Prices and Particulars of " Studio Boxes,"

see pages 17 *and* 18.

STUDIO BOX, No. 4.

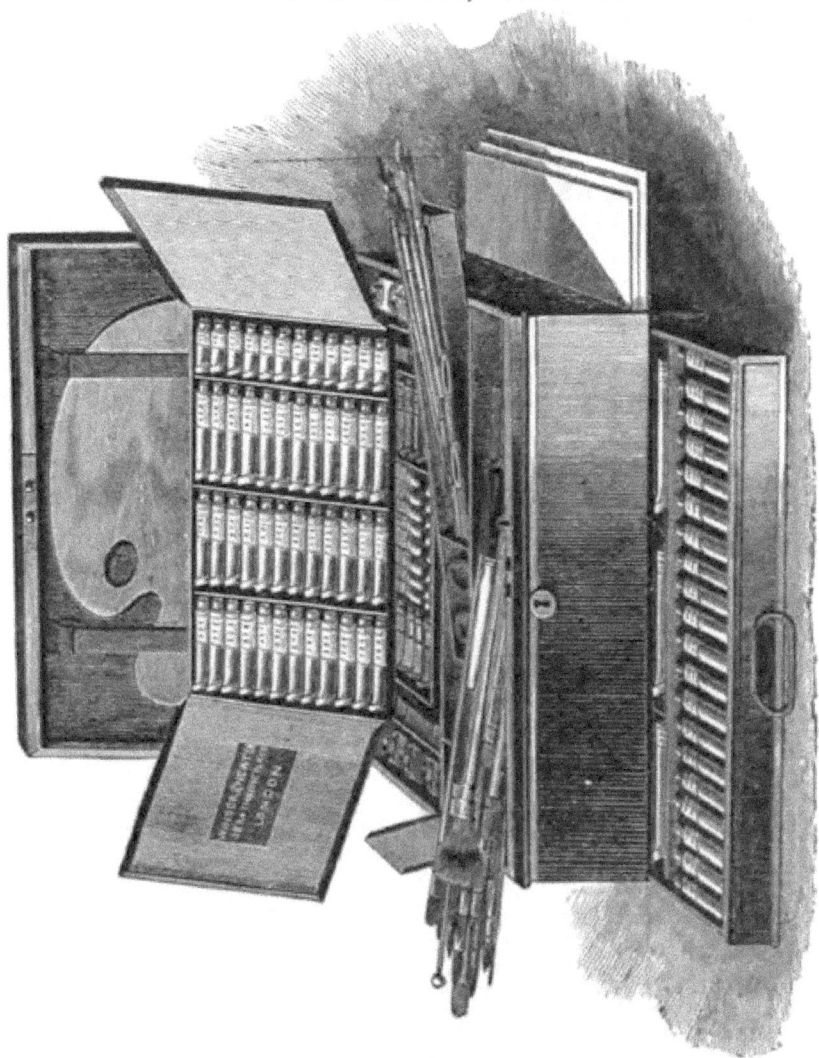

(For Prices and Particulars see page 18).

COMPANION BOX. *(Illustrated at page 12.)*
Price £1 11s. 6d.—fitted complete. (Empty Box, 9s.)

COMPANION BOX: Size 13 inches by 9, 1½ inch deep: containing twenty Colours, Sable and Hog-hair Brushes, Badger Softener, Chalk, Portcrayon, Palette Knife, Dipper, Oil, Turpentine and Mahogany Palette.

PORTABLE BOX. *(Illustrated at page 12).*
Price £2 2s.—fitted complete. (Empty Box, 12s.)

PORTABLE BOX: Size 13¾ inches by 9, 1½ inch deep: containing twenty-two Colours, a general selection of Sable and Hog-hair Brushes, Badger Softener, Chalk, Portcrayon, Oil and Turpentine, Palette Knife, Capped Dipper and Mahogany Palette.

DOUBLE PORTABLE BOX. *(Illustrated at page 13.)*
Price £2 12s. 6d.—fitted complete. (Empty Box, 16s.)

DOUBLE PORTABLE BOX: Size 13½ incues by 9, 2½ inches deep: containing twenty-four Colours, a general selection of Sable and Hog-hair Brushes, Badger Softener, Chalk, Portcrayon, Palette Knife, Capped Dipper, Oil, Turpentine, Mahogany Palette and three Prepared Boards 13 inches by 8.

ACADEMY BOX. *(Illustrated at page 13.)*
Price £3 3s.—fitted complete. (Empty Box, 19s. 6d.)

ACADEMY BOX: Size 12¼ inches by 9, 4½ inches deep: containing thirty Colours, with a general selection of Sable and Hog-hair Brushes, Badger Softener, Chalk, Charcoal, Portcrayon, Palette Knife, Double Capped Dipper, Varnish, Oil, Turpentine, Mahogany Palette and three Prepared Boards, 12 inches by 8.

STUDIO BOX, No. 1. *(Illustrated at page 14).*
Price £3 13s. 6d.—fitted complete. (Empty Box, £1 5s.)

STUDIO BOX, No. 1: Size 12¾ inches by 10, 4 inches deep: containing thirty-two Colours, with a general selection of Sable and Hog-hair Brushes, Badger Softener, Chalk, Portcrayon, Steel and Ivory Palette Knives, Capped Dipper, Mastic Varnish, Pale Drying Oil, Linseed Oil, Turpentine, Mahogany Palette and three Prepared Boards, 12 inches by 9.

c

STUDIO BOX, No. 2.   (*Illustrated at page* 14).

Price £5 5*s.*—fitted complete.   (Empty Box, £1 11*s.* 6*d.*)

STUDIO BOX, No. 2 : Size 15 inches by 11, 4 inches deep: containing forty Colours, with a general selection of Sable and Hog-hair Brushes, Badger Softener, Chalk, Charcoal, Portcrayon, Steel and Ivory Palette Knives, Double Capped Dipper, Mastic Varnish, Pale Drying Oil, Linseed Oil, Turpentine, Mahogany Palette, and three Prepared Boards, 14 inches by 10.

STUDIO BOX, No. 3.   (*Illustrated at page* 15).

Price £12 12*s.*—fitted complete.   (Empty Box, with Brush Washer and two Rimmed Dippers, £3 10*s.*)

STUDIO BOX, No. 3 : Size 17¾ inches by 12¼, 5¼ inches deep : containing sixty Colours, with a general selection of Sable and Hog-hair Brushes, Badger Softener, Chalk, Charcoal, Portcrayon, Steel and Ivory Palette Knives, Oil Scraper, Double Capped and Rimmed Dippers, Jointed Mahl Stick, Mastic and Picture Copal Varnishes, Turpentine, Pale Drying, Linseed, and Poppy Oils, Mahogany Palette and three Prepared Boards, 17 inches by 12. Also the following Powder Colours in Bottles : Lemon Yellow, Fine Crimson Lake, Orient Carmine, Rose Madder and Fine French Ultramarine.

STUDIO BOX, No. 4.   (*Illustrated at page* 16.)

Price £26 5*s.*—fitted complete. (Empty Box, with Smudge Pan, six Japanned Oil Bottles, Brush Washer and two Rimmed Dippers, £8 10*s.*)

STUDIO BOX, No. 4 : Size 20 inches by 14, 8¼ inches deep: containing eighty-four Colours, *with a complete assortment of Materials ;* comprising Flat, Round, Rigger, Bright's, and Fan Sable Brushes ; Flat and Round Hog-hair Brushes, Flat and Round Extra Fine ditto, Landseer's, Bright's, and Fan ditto, Flat Varnish Brush, Badger Softeners, Chalk, Charcoal, Portcrayons, Steel and Ivory Palette Knives, Scraper, Artist's Pocket Knife, Brush Washer, Smudge Pan, Capped and Rimmed Dippers, Ground Glass Slab and Mullers, China Slabs for submerging Colours, large and small Artist's Gallipots, ¼-pint each Mastic and Picture Copal Varnishes, Turpentine, Pale Drying, Linseed, and Poppy Oils, six Japanned Bottles for ditto with screw tops, three Prepared Boards, 19 inches by 13, Mahogany Palette and Jointed Mahl Stick. And the following Powder Colours in Bottles: Aureolin, Lemon Yellow, Fine Crimson Lake, Orient Carmine, Madder Carmine, Cobalt, Fine French Ultramarine and Genuine Ultramarine.

WINSOR & NEWTON'S

ARTISTS' CANVAS.

The best British-made Canvas of pure Flax, and the purest materials only, are used by WINSOR & NEWTON, Limited, in the production of their Artists' Prepared Canvas.

The space afforded by their new Factory, the extensive plant contained therein, and their staff of trained skilled workmen, enable them to execute all orders with dispatch.

The superior method of manufacture adopted by WINSOR & NEWTON, Limited, materially enhances the quality of their Artists' Canvas. *It is dried naturally and without the aid of artificial means;* and the adhesion of the surface of preparation to the ground of raw Canvas is so intimate and thorough, as to preclude the possibility of its peeling up or becoming detached in any way.

c 2

WINSOR & NEWTON'S

ARTISTS' CANVAS.

Prepared on the Best Linen Fabric.

IN ROLLS OF SIX YARDS.						Roman or Plain Canvas. s. d.	Ticken. s. d.
27 inches wide	...	...	...	... per yard		2 9	3 6
30 ,, ,,	...	...	...	... ,,		3 0	3 9
36 ,, ,,	...	...	...	... ,,		3 6	4 6
38 ,, ,,	...	...	...	... ,,		3 9	5 0
3 feet 6 inches wide	...	...	...	,,		4 6	5 6
3 ,, 9 ,, ,,	...	...	...	,,		5 3	6 3
4 ,, 6 ,, ,,	...	...	...	,,		6 9	7 6
5 ,, 2 ,, ,,	...		...	,,		8 0	10 0
6 ,, 2 ,, ,,	...	...	...	,,		10 0	11 6
7 ,, 2 ,, ,,	...	...	...	,,		12 0	14 6

OIL SKETCHING PAPERS.

					s. d.
Oil Sketching Paper, 30 inches by 22 ...	... per sheet				0 9
Ditto, Extra Stout, 30 ,, 22 ...	... ,,				1 0

ACADEMY BOARDS.

						s. d.
Academy Boards	...	24¼ inches by 18¼	...	... each		1 0
Half ditto	...	18¼ ,, 12¼	...	... ,,		0 6
Quarto ditto	...	12¼ ,, 9¼	...	... ,,		0 3
Thick Academy Boards	24¼ ,, 18¼		...	... ,,		1 3
Half ditto	...	18¼ ,, 12¼	...	... ,,		0 8
Quarto ditto	...	12¼ ,, 9¼	...	... ,,		0 4

WINSOR & NEWTON'S

ROMAN OR PLAIN CANVAS ON WEDGED FRAMES.

Size in Inches.	Each. s. d.	Size in Inches.	Each. s. d.
8 by 6	0 8	22 by 14	2 3
9 „ 6	0 9	22 „ 16	2 3
9 „ 7	0 10	22 „ 18	2 6
10 „ 6	0 10	24 „ 12	2 1
10 „ 7	0 11	24 „ 14	2 3
10 „ 8	1 0	24 „ 16	2 6
11 „ 9	1 1	24 „ 18	2 9
12 „ 6	0 11	24 „ 20	3 0
12 „ 8	1 0	26 „ 16	2 10
12 „ 9	1 1	26 „ 18	3 0
12 „ 10	1 2	26 „ 20	3 3
13 „ 9	1 2	26 „ 22	3 6
13 „ 10	1 3	27 „ 20	3 3
13 „ 11	1 3	27 „ 22	3 7
14 „ 7	1 1	30 „ 18	3 6
14 „ 8	1 2	30 „ 20	3 8
14 „ 9	1 3	30 „ 22	4 0
14 „ 10	1 3	30 „ 24	4 2
14 „ 12	1 4	30 „ 25	4 3
15 „ 11	1 5	36 „ 20	4 4
15 „ 12	1 6	36 „ 24	5 0
16 „ 8	1 3	36 „ 28	5 6
16 „ 10	1 5	40 „ 24	6 0
16 „ 12	1 6	40 „ 28	7 0
16 „ 14	1 9	40 „ 30	8 0
17 „ 13	1 9	42 „ 24	6 6
17 „ 14	1 9	42 „ 28	7 6
18 „ 10	1 6	44 „ 34 Small Half	
18 „ 12	1 8	Length	9 6
18 „ 14	1 10	50 „ 30 Landscape	10 6
18 „ 16	2 0	50 „ 40 Half Length	12 6
19 „ 13	1 10	56 „ 44 Bishop's Half	
19 „ 15	2 0	Length	16 6
20 „ 12	1 10	88 „ 52 Small Whole	
20 „ 14	2 0	Length	32 0
20 „ 15	2 0	94 „ 58 Whole Length	42 0
20 „ 16	2 1	106 „ 70 Bishop's Whole	
21 „ 14	2 0	Length	54 0
21 „ 17	2 3		

Stretchers covered with Ticken at proportionate Prices.

MILLBOARDS AND MAHOGANY PANELS.

With carefully prepared surfaces for painting on.

Size in Inches.	Prepared Millboards. Each. s. d.	Prepared Panels. Each. s. d.	Size in Inches.	Prepared Millboards. Each. s. d.	Prepared Panels. Each. s. d.
6 by 5 ...	0 6	—	17 by 12 ...	2 0	5 3
7 ,, 5 ...	0 7	—	17 ,, 13*...	2 3	5 6
8 ,, 6 ...	0 8	1 3	17 ,, 14 ...	2 4	6 0
9 ,, 6*...	0 8	1 6	18 ,, 12*...	2 3	5 6
9 ,, 7 ...	0 9	1 6	18 ,, 13 ...	2 4	6 0
9 ,, 8 ...	0 9	—	18 ,, 14 ...	2 6	6 6
10 ,, 7*...	0 9	1 9	19 ,, 12 ...	2 6	—
10 ,, 8*...	0 10	2 0	19 ,, 13*...	2 6	6 6
11 ,, 8*...	0 10	2 3	19 ,, 14 ...	2 8	7 0
11 ,, 9*...	1 0	2 6	20 ,, 14*...	2 10	7 6
12 ,, 8*...	1 0	2 8	20 ,, 15 ...	—	8 3
12 ,, 9*...	1 1	3 0	20 ,, 16 ...	3 2	9 0
12 ,, 10*...	1 1	3 3	21 ,, 14 ...	—	8 6
13 ,, 8*...	1 1	3 0	21 ,, 15 ...	3 3	—
13 ,, 9 ...	1 1	3 3	21 ,, 17 ...	3 9	10 6
13 ,, 10*...	1 2	3 6	22 ,, 15 ...	3 6	—
13 ,, 11 ...	1 3	3 9	22 ,, 16 ...	3 9	10 6
14 ,, 9 ...	1 3	3 6	22 ,, 18 ...	4 6	12 0
14 ,, 10*...	1 3	3 9	23 ,, 16 ...	4 0	11 6
14 ,, 12*...	1 6	4 6	24 ,, 18 ...	5 3	13 0
15 ,, 11*...	1 8	4 6	24 ,, 20 ...	6 0	14 0
15 ,, 12 ...	1 9	4 9	30 ,, 20 ...	—	21 0
16 ,, 11 ..	1 9	4 9	30 ,, 25 ...	9 0	27 0
16 ,, 12*...	1 10	5 0	36 ,, 28 ...	—	36 0

*CANVAS BOARDS.—Plain Millboards covered with prepared Artists' Canvas are now made in the sizes marked with a star, at the prices of the prepared Millboards above.

SOLID BLOCKS FOR SKETCHING IN OIL.

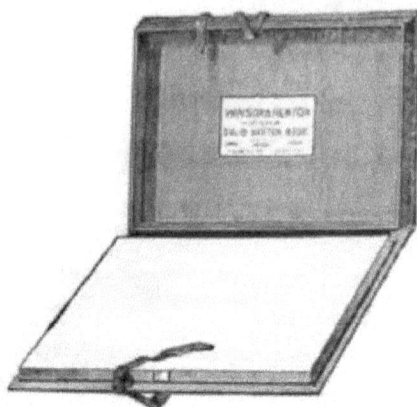

Solid Blocks of Extra Thick Prepared Paper, containing 24 sheets, have been made to avoid the weight and expense of those with 32.

	Inches.	Thick Paper, containing 32 sheets.		Extra Thick Paper, containing 24 sheets.	
		Blocks only.	Half Bound and with Protective Frames.	Blocks only.	Half Bound and with Protective Frames.
		s. d.	s. d.	s. d.	s. d.
16mo. Imperial,	7 by 5 each	2 3	4 6	2 3	4 6
8vo. ,,	10 ,, 7 ,,	4 0	7 6	4 0	7 6
6mo. ,,	14 ,, 6½ ,,	5 6	10 6	5 6	10 6
4to. ,,	14 ,, 10 ,,	7 6	13 0	7 6	13 0
3mo. ,,	18 ,, 10 ,,	—	—	11 0	19 0
Half ,,	20 ,, 14 ,,	—	—	16 0	26 0

GROUND GLASS SLABS & MULLERS.

Glass Slabs.

Inches.		Glass Slabs only.	Set in Mahogany Frames.
		s. d.	s. d.
6 × 6	each	1 0	3 0
8 × 8	,,	1 6	4 0
10 × 10	,,	2 6	5 0
12 × 12	,,	3 6	6 0

Glass Mullers.

			s. d
1 inch diameter . each			0 6
1½ ,, ,, . ,,			0 8
2 ,, ,, . ,,			0 9
2½ ,, ,, . ,,			1 0
3 ,, ,, . ,,			1 6
4 ,, ,, . ,,			1 9

WINSOR & NEWTON'S
SABLE BRUSHES IN TIN FERRULES,
FOR OIL PAINTING.
WITH 12-INCH POLISHED RED CEDAR HANDLES.

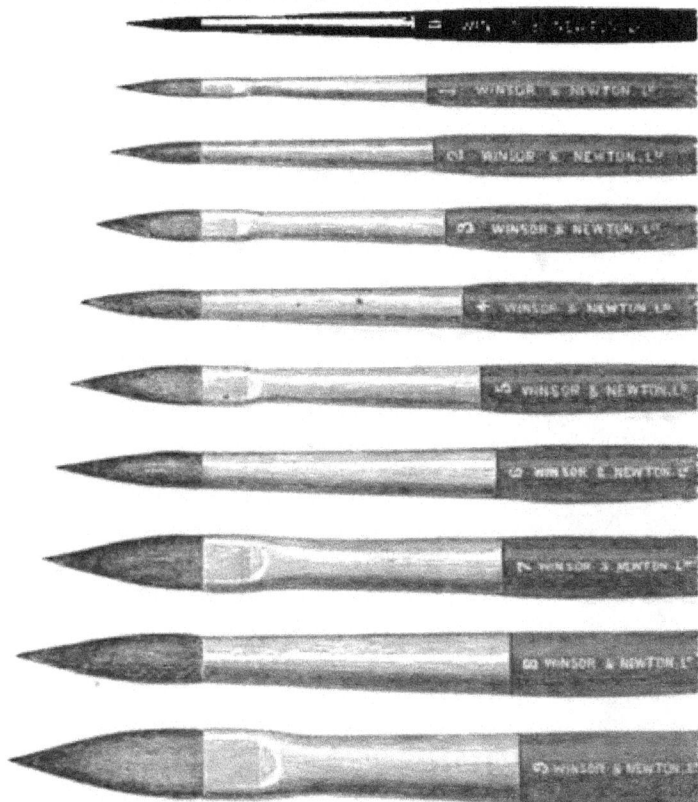

FLAT OR ROUND.				FLAT.			*s.*	*d.*
			s.	*d.*	No. 7 ...	... ... each	1	9
Nos. 0 and 1 ...	... each	0	6	„ 8 ...	... ... „	2	4
„ 2	... ... „	0	7	„ 9 ...	... ... „	3	0
„ 3	... ... „	0	9	„ 10 ...	... ... „	3	6
„ 4	... ... „	1	0	ROUND.				
„ 5	... ... „	1	2	No. 7 ...	... ... each	2	3
„ 6	... ... „	1	4	„ 8 ...	... ... „	3	0
				„ 9 ...	... ... „	3	6

WINSOR & NEWTON'S

HOG HAIR BRUSHES IN TIN FERRULES,

FOR OIL PAINTING.

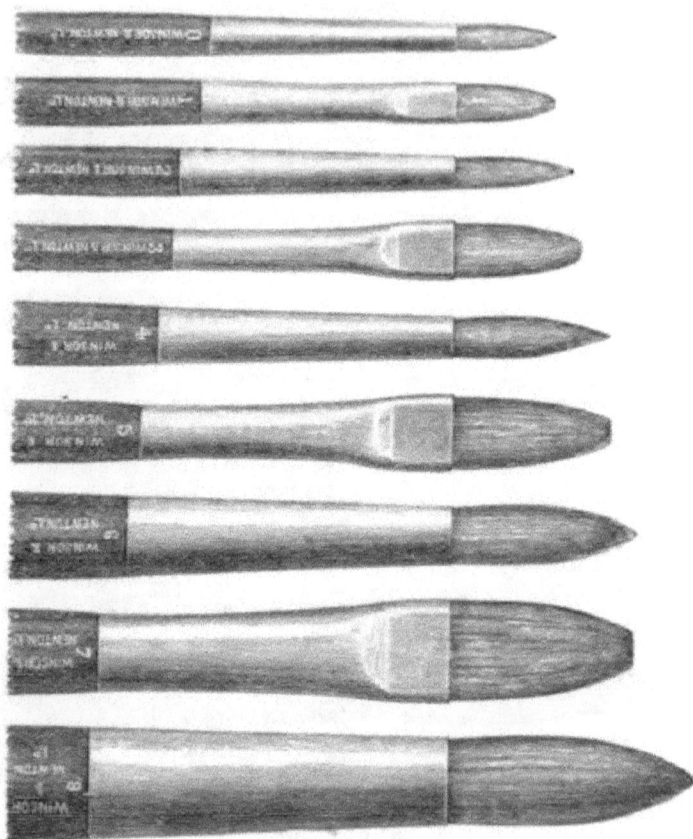

For prices and particulars see next page.

WINSOR & NEWTON'S

HOG HAIR BRUSHES IN TIN FERRULES,

FOR OIL PAINTING.

WITH 12-INCH POLISHED RED CEDAR HANDLES.

FLAT OR ROUND.

	s. d.		s. d.		s. d.
No. 1 to 6 each	0 4	No. 11 ... each	0 10	No. 15 ... each	2 0
,, 7 ... ,,	0 6	,, 12 ... ,,	1 0	,, 16 ... ,,	2 3
,, 8 ... ,,	0 7	,, 13 ... ,,	1 6	,, 17 ... ,,	2 6
,, 9 ... ,,	0 8	,, 14 ... ,,	1 9	,, 18 ... ,,	2 9
,, 10 ... ,,	0 9				

WINSOR & NEWTON'S

EXTRA FINE

HOG-HAIR BRUSHES IN TIN FERRULES.

WITH 12-INCH POLISHED YELLOW HANDLES.

Made of the finest and softest Lyons Hog Hair, feather-edged, and graduated so as to blend and keep well together in working. These Brushes range between Sable and the ordinary Hog-hair Brushes, combining somewhat of the softness of the former with the firmness of the latter.

FLAT OR ROUND.

	s. d.		s. d.		s. d.
No. 1 to 6 each	0 8	No. 9 ... each	1 2	No. 11 ... each	1 6
,, 7 ... ,,	0 9	,, 10 ... ,,	1 4	,, 12 ... ,,	1 9
,, 8 ,,	1 0				

For Illustrations of the above Brushes see preceding page.

WINSOR & NEWTON'S
HOG HAIR BRUSHES IN TIN FERRULES,

SHORT AND THIN IN HAIR.

With 12-inch "Unpolished Pine" Handles.

"Flat only." Nos. 1 to 6, all sizes, 2d. each.

No.				s.	d.	No.					s.	d.
7	...	...	... each	0	3	10	...	...	... each		0	6
8	...	...	... „	0	4	11	...	...	... „		0	7
9	...	...	... „	0	5	12	...	...	... „		0	8

FLAT HOG HAIR VARNISHING BRUSHES IN TIN FERRULES.

SPECIAL MAKE.—SOFTEST LYONS HAIR.

With Polished Cedar Handles.

			s.	d.				s.	d.
1 inch wide	... each		1	3	3 inches wide	... each		3	6
1½ „	...	... „	1	9	3½ „	...	... „	4	0
2 „	...	„	2	3	4 „	...	... „	4	6
2½ „	...	... „	3	0					

"FAN" SHAPE BRUSHES IN TIN FERRULES.

Containing little hair, and adapted for light touching, fur, foliage, herbage, &c.

With 12-inch Yellow Handles.

		Made of Sable Hair.		Made of Softest Lyons Hair.	
		s.	d.	s.	d.
Nos 1, 2, and 3	... each	1	9	0	9
„ 4, 5, and 6	... „	2	3	1	0

FINEST ROUND BADGER HAIR SOFTENERS.
Red Polished Handles.

No.				s.	d.	No.				s.	d.
1	...	...	... each	0	9	7	...	...	... each	3	6
2	...	...	... „	1	0	8	...	...	... „	4	0
3	...	...	... „	1	6	9	...	...	... „	5	0
4	...	...	... „	2	0	10	...	...	... „	6	0
5	...	...	... „	2	6	11	...	...	... „	7	0
6	...	...	... „	3	0	12	...	...	... „	8	0

POONAH BRUSHES.
With 6-inch Polished Red Handles.

		s.	d.
POONAH BRUSHES, Nos. 1 to 6 ...	each	0	4

WINSOR & NEWTON'S

DIPPERS

FOR OIL AND WATER COLOUR PAINTING.

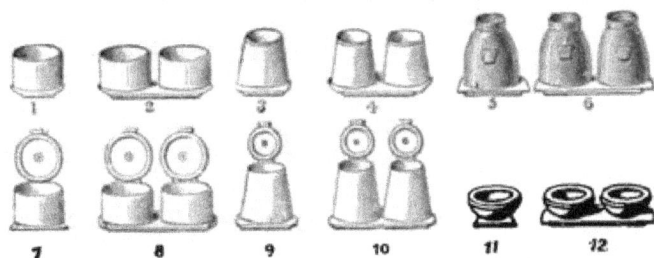

			Plain Tin.		Japanned.	
			s.	d.	s.	d.
No. 1.	Tin Dippers ... ... each		0	3	0	5
,, 2.	Ditto, Double ... ... ,,		0	5	0	9
,, 3.	Conical Tin Dippers ... ... ,,		0	5	0	6
,, 4.	Ditto, Double ... ... ,,		0	8	1	0
,, 5.	Water Colour Dippers with necks for corks ... ... ,,		—		0	8
,, 6.	Ditto, Double ... ... ,,		—		1	3
,, 7.	Capped Tin Dippers ... ... ,,		0	9	—	
,, 8.	Ditto, Double ... ... ,,		1	6	—	
,, 9.	Capped Conical Tin Dippers ... ,,		0	8	—	
,, 10.	Ditto, Double ... ... ,,		1	6	—	
,, 11.	Improved Dippers with moveable rims ,,		0	6	0	10
,, 12.	Ditto, Double ... ... ,,		1	2	1	9

TIN WARE SUNDRIES.

		s.	d.
Japanned Tin flat Oil Bottles with screw tops ... each		1	9
Brush Washers, round at top, plain Tin ... ... ,,		1	9
,, ,, ,, ,, japanned Tin ... ... ,,		2	0
Improved Square Brush Washers, plain Tin ... ... ,,		2	6
,, ,, ,, ,, japanned Tin ... ,,		3	0
Smudge Pans, 14 inches long, plain Tin ... ,,		2	8
Improved Smudge Pans, 14 inches long, plain Tin ... ,,		3	9
Round Japanned Cases, to contain Oil Painting Brushes, 13 inches long by 1¼ diameter ... ,,		1	6
Ditto 14 inches long by 2 diameter ... ... ,,		1	9

STEEL PALETTE KNIVES.

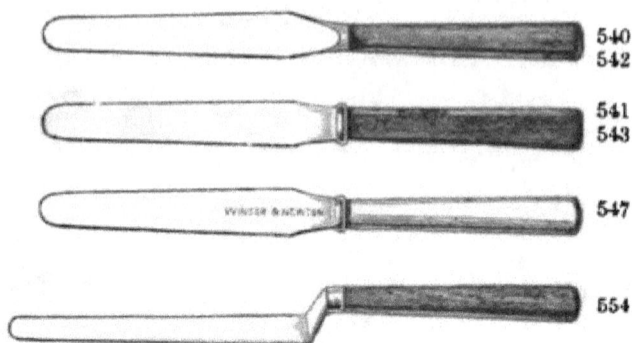

540
542

541
543

547

554

Palette Knives of various shapes and lengths of Blade,
from 8*d*. to 3*s*. each.

SCRAPERS AND ERASERS.

No. 1.	No. 2.	No. 3.	No. 4.	No. 5.
6*d*.	2*s*. 3*d*.	1*s*.	1*s*. 2*d*.	1*s*. 6*d*.

Scrapers and Erasers, from 6*d*. to 2*s*. 3*d*. each.

EASELS.

WINSOR & NEWTON'S

IMPROVED STUDIO EASELS.

See Illustration on following page.

WINSOR & NEWTON'S IMPROVED STUDIO EASEL will carry canvases of any size to ten feet in height. The arrangement for projecting a canvas in a forward position is simple and effective; and the Easel has a screw (winding-up) movement, that is managed with the utmost facility, and which raises with ease, a Picture or canvas of great weight.

Among the many purchasers of WINSOR & NEWTON'S IMPROVED STUDIO EASELS may be mentioned the names of the following Artists and Amateurs of eminence, viz. :—

Alma-Tadema,L.,Esq.,R.A.	Faed, T., Esq., R.A.	Roberts, D., R.A., the late
Amiconi, B., the late	Fildes, S. L., Esq., A.R.A.	Rossetti, D. G., the late
Ansdell, R., Esq., R.A.	Girardot, E. G., Esq.	Sant, James, Esq., R.A.
Brett, J., Esq., A.R.A.	Graves, The Hon. H.,the late	Selous, H. C., Esq.
Buckner, R., the late	Haden, F. Seymour, Esq.	Swinton, J. R., Esq.
Calderon, P. H., Esq., R.A.	Hunt, W. Holman, Esq.	Tayler, Frederick, Esq.
Chester, G., Esq.	Knight, J. P., R.A.,the late	Thomas, W. Cave, Esq.
Cole, Vicat, Esq., R.A.	Leech, John, the late	Walton, Elijah, the late
Collinson, R., Esq.	Leighton,Sir Fredk.,P.R.A.	Walton, J. W., Esq.
Corbould, E., Esq.	Linnell, W., Esq.	Warren, Edmund, Esq.
Davis, H. W. B., Esq., R.A.	Naish, J. G., Esq.	Watson, J. D., Esq.
Desanges, L. W., Esq.	Philip, John, R.A., the late	Watts, G. F., Esq., R.A.
Dowling, R., Esq.	Pinwell, G., the late	Whistler, J., Esq.
Elmore, A., R.A., the late	Poole, P. F., R.A., the late	Wilson, Herbert, Esq.

	£	s.	d.
Small Studio Easel in Stained Deal 5 feet high	11	11	0
Middle ,, ,, 6 ,, ...	12	12	0
Large ,, ,, 7 ,, ...	13	13	0
Small Studio Easel in Polished Oak 5 ,, ...	14	14	0
Middle ,, ,, 6 ,, ...	15	15	0
Large ,, ,, 7 ,, ...	17	17	0

ILLUSTRATION OF

WINSOR & NEWTON'S

IMPROVED STUDIO EASEL.

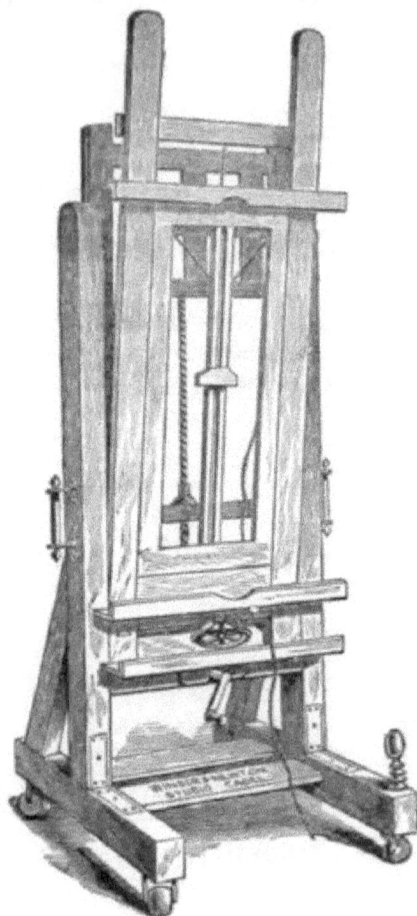

ILLUSTRATIONS OF

WINSOR & NEWTON'S

EASELS.

CORBOULD EASELS.

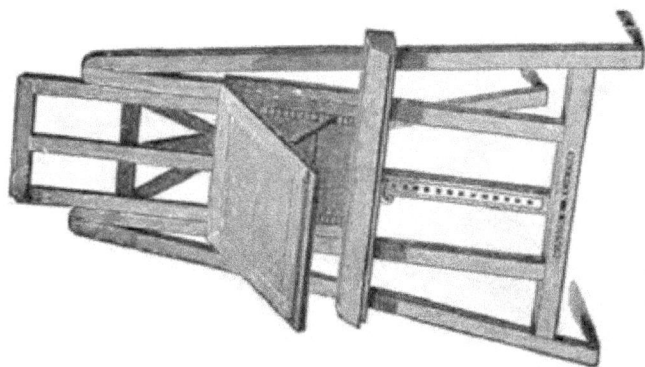

MAHOGANY CORBOULD EASEL.
WITHOUT DESK.
No. 13.—6 feet high, 3 feet 2 inches wide at base.

MAHOGANY CORBOULD EASEL.
WITH DESK COMPLETE.
No. 14.—6 feet high, 3 feet 2 inches wide at base.

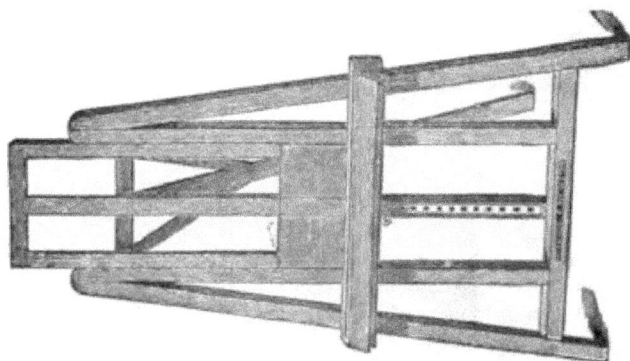

BACK EASELS.

ACADEMY EASEL.

MAHOGANY BACK EASEL
WITH TRAY.
No. 10.—6 *feet high,*
3 feet 3 inches wide.

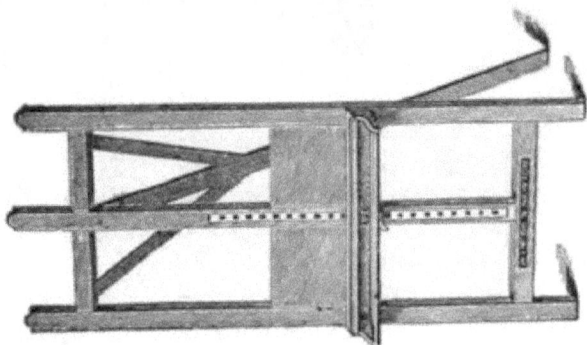

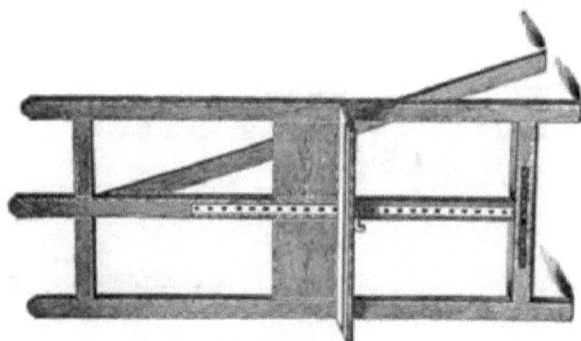

MAHOGANY BACK EASEL
WITH BRUSH BOX.
No. 11.—6 *feet high,*
3 feet 3 inches wide.
(For Prices see following page.)

MAHOGANY BACK ACADEMY
EASEL.
No. 12.—6 *feet high,*
3 feet 8 inches wide.